Social Studies

Grades K–1

The best social studies activities and reproducibles from the 1996–2002 issues of *The Mailbox®* magazine

- **All About Me**
- **Building Character**
- **Family**
- **Homes**
- **Patriotism**

- **Careers**
- **Maps and Geography**
- **Transportation**
- **Holidays and Celebrations**

Editorial Team: Becky S. Andrews, Kimberley Bruck, Karen P. Shelton, Diane Badden, Thad H. McLaurin, Sharon Murphy, Debra Liverman, Karen A. Brudnak, Sarah Hamblet, Hope Rodgers, Dorothy C. McKinney

Production Team: Lisa K. Pitts, Pam Crane, Rebecca Saunders, Jennifer Tipton Cappoen, Chris Curry, Sarah Foreman, Theresa Lewis Goode, Clint Moore, Greg D. Rieves, Barry Slate, Donna K. Teal, Zane Williard, Tazmen Carlisle, Irene Harvley-Felder, Amy Kirtley-Hill, Kristy Parton, Cathy Edwards Simrell, Lynette Dickerson, Mark Rainey

www.themailbox.com

Manufactured in the United States
10 9 8 7 6 5 4 3 2

Table of Contents

All About Me
Special You, Special Me! 4
Everybody Has Feelings.. 10

Building Character 15

Family
Families Are Fun!.. 32
A Family Affair 36
An Event to Remember 40

Homes
There's No Place Like Home 44
Right at Home.. 48

Careers
When I Grow Up 54

Maps and Geography
Once Upon a Map… 70

Transportation
Keep on Truckin'.. 78
Cruisin' Across the Curriculum 80

Patriotism
Hooray for the USA! 86
Red, White, & Blue Review 90
Positively Presidential.. 92

Holidays and Celebrations
Thanksgiving Remembered.. 98
Winter Celebrations 104
Cinco de Mayo... 109

All About Me

Special You, Special Me!

Snowflakes and children are both one of a kind. This blizzard of activities focuses on self-esteem and will help your youngsters see that to be different is to be special.

ideas contributed by Susan A. DeRiso, Carole Dibble, and Kathy Lee

A Special Sharing

Celebrate the uniqueness of each student during circle time with this special touch. In advance, create this snowflake wand using a sheet of one-inch foam, a 12-inch wooden dowel, two wiggle eyes, and red felt. To make the wand, use a serrated knife to cut out a snowflake from the foam. If desired, use the pattern on page 7 as a template. Insert the dowel into the bottom of the snowflake to create a handle. Then glue on the wiggle eyes and a felt mouth as shown.

Have students pass the wand around the circle while singing the tune below. Encourage the child holding the wand at the end of the verse to share something special about himself. Continue singing the verse until each child has had a turn to share.

I'm Something Special
(sung to the tune of "London Bridge")

Share with us some special news,
Special news, special news.
Share with us some special news
About you!

Pam Crane

Fingerprinting Flurry

Frolicking fingers make a flurry of snow in this activity. Explain to your little ones that fingerprints and snowflakes are similar because there are no two flakes nor fingerprints that are exactly alike. Give each child a sheet of dark-colored construction paper and provide access to white washable paint. Demonstrate how to draw on the paper several lines that intersect at the same point. Encourage the child to use the lines as guides and make fingerprints (or use toes!) along and beside the lines to create her own unique snowflake. Cut out the flakes and display them together with the title "A Flurry of Fun!"

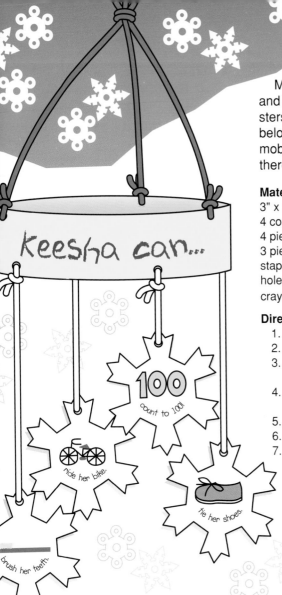

A Snowstorm of Successes

Many things make us unique. Often we are differentiated by things we can and cannot do. By focusing on the *cans* with this snowy mobile, your youngsters will be shoveling up mounds of self-esteem. Gather the materials listed below. Then assist each child in completing the directions. Hang the finished mobiles from your ceiling to create a constant reminder of "I can!" Wow, there's a real feeling of success in the air!

Materials for each student:
3" x 24" tagboard strip
4 copies of the snowflake pattern on page 7
4 pieces of white yarn cut in different lengths
3 pieces of blue yarn cut the same length
stapler
hole puncher
crayons

Directions:
1. Write your name and "can…" on the tagboard strip.
2. Staple the ends of the strip together to form a cylinder.
3. Punch four holes around the bottom of the cylinder and three holes around the top.
4. On each snowflake, write/dictate and illustrate a different activity that you can complete successfully.
5. Cut out the snowflakes and then punch a hole at the top of each one.
6. Attach each snowflake to the bottom of the cylinder with a white piece of yarn.
7. Tie one end of each piece of blue yarn to a different hole in the top of the cylinder; then tie the loose ends together.

A Blizzard of Praise

Shake up spirits with these rewarding jars of praise. In advance, collect a class supply of clean baby food jars (with the labels removed). Also, duplicate and cut out the snowflake pattern on this page for each child.

To make a praise jar, cut a child's photo to fit the inside of the jar's lid. Then laminate the photo and hot-glue it to the inside of the lid. Next, fill the jar with water, add some silver glitter, and secure the lid. Finally, glue the snowflake to the top of the lid.

Keep the jars on students' desks or tables and use them as magical, motivating rewards. To give praise and attention to a deserving child, simply turn his jar upside down. Now that's something to cheer about!

Double the Pleasure, Double the Fun

This version of the traditional memory game gets up close and personal to help students refine their visual-discrimination skills. To prepare the game, duplicate the snowflake cards on page 8 on tagboard and then cut them apart. Make two copies of each child's photograph. Cut out the duplicated photos and mount them on the tagboard cards. Mix the cards together and arrange them facedown on a tabletop. (If there are too many cards, divide them to make two games.) Then invite each child in a small group to try to find a matching pair. Look carefully!

Snowflake Pattern

Hooray for ME!

Snowflake Snacks

Your little ones will love creating these uniquely different treats. Gather the ingredients and supplies listed below. Have each child place part of a doily on top of her cupcake. Then help her sift powdered sugar over the doily. Carefully remove it to reveal a snowflake design. No two treats will be the same!

Ingredients/supplies needed:
chocolate cupcake for each child
powdered sugar
sifter
doilies

If You Were a Snowflake...

Hmmm, what would you do? Youngsters will have no trouble pretending to be snowflakes in this creative-thinking activity. Duplicate page 9 for each child. Pose the question "What do snowflakes do?" during a group time and brainstorm the possibilities. Have each child imagine that he is a snowflake and record his dictation on his page. Encourage the child to illustrate his story. Then bind the completed pages together to make a class book. Share the stories during the next circle time, being sure to acknowledge the author-illustrator of each page.

If I were a snowflake...

I'd whirl right to the tip of my mom's nose!

by David

Sing a Song of Self-Esteem

Now that your youngsters know that being different makes them special, they have something to sing about! So teach this little ditty and sing up a snowstorm.

(sung to the tune of "She'll Be Comin' Round the Mountain")

We all are very different, yes, we know.
Yes, we know! *(shout)*
We all are very different, yes, we know.
Yes, we know! *(shout)*
From our heads down to our toes—
Like the little flakes of snow—
We all are very different, yes, we know.
Yes, we know! *(shout)*

Use with "A Special Sharing" on page 4 and "A Snowstorm of Successes" on page 5.

Snowflake Cards
Use with "Double the Pleasure, Double the Fun" on page 5.

If I were a snowflake...

by

_____

Everybody Has Feelings

Here's a unit full of ideas to help your little ones begin to label, communicate, and understand feelings. Whether they're feeling happy, sad, silly, or frustrated, your students will learn to express and accept their own feelings with the help of the activities in this unit.

ideas contributed by Lucia Kemp Henry and Lori Kent

Let's Talk About Feelings

Begin to focus on feelings by reading aloud *Proud of Our Feelings* by Lindsay Leghorn. Afterward, ask students to recall some of the feelings mentioned in this book. Use this discussion time to introduce and reinforce new vocabulary words associated with feelings. Next, invite students to dramatize how they would feel in a variety of situations by using questions like the ones below. Encourage each child to act out her reaction. Then challenge that student to name that emotional feeling. Follow up this activity by teaching students the song in "Sing a Song of Feelings" on this page.

- How would you feel if you opened a present and it was just what you've always wanted?
- How would you feel if your favorite pet were lost?
- How would you feel if you were lost in a dark forest?
- How would you feel if you had nothing to do on a cold, rainy day?

Sing a Song of Feelings

Help your youngsters learn to identify and express their feelings with this song. Invite students to use their voices along with body language to dramatize the suggested feeling in the song. Then repeat the song, substituting a different feeling each time. In no time at all, your little ones will be singing about feelings!

I Have Feelings
(sung to the tune of "Frère Jacques")

I have feelings; I have feelings.
Look at me and you'll see.
Sometimes I feel [mad],
Really, really [mad].
Look at me and you'll see.

What Are You Feeling?

Once your youngsters have identified some feelings in themselves, help them learn to "read" the feelings of others. In advance, cut out magazine pictures of people expressing emotions. Glue each picture onto a separate sheet of construction paper. Compile the pages into a book; then staple them between two construction paper covers. Title the book "A Book of Feelings." To use the book, share it with students during a group time. Ask children to study a picture; then invite them to tell what they think that person is feeling. Encourage them to suggest a reason or cause for that feeling. There are great opportunities for assessment here since students will, no doubt, be sharing important information about their own feelings.

"I Have Feelings" Booklet

Your little ones will flip to share their many feeling faces after making this booklet. Prepare by cutting a 7½" x 9½" construction paper back page for each child. Then reproduce the booklet page pattern on page 14 two times. Program one of these copies with the title "I Have Feelings." Program the other copy with "Sometimes I feel." Then, for each child, reproduce one booklet cover and four booklet pages.

To make the booklet:

1. Have a child cut out one booklet page. Encourage her to color or glue art supplies on her cutout to resemble her own hair. Have the child write a feeling word in the space provided, then color facial features to match that emotion. Glue this cutout to the back construction paper page so that the bottom edges are even.

2. For each subsequent page, have the child cut out the booklet page, write a feeling word, and illustrate the face with that feeling.

3. Encourage each child to color the booklet cover to resemble herself.

4. Have each child stack the back page and three pages, placing the cover on top. Then instruct her to staple her booklet together along the bottom edge.

After sharing these booklets as a class, encourage each child to take her booklet home to share her feelings with her family.

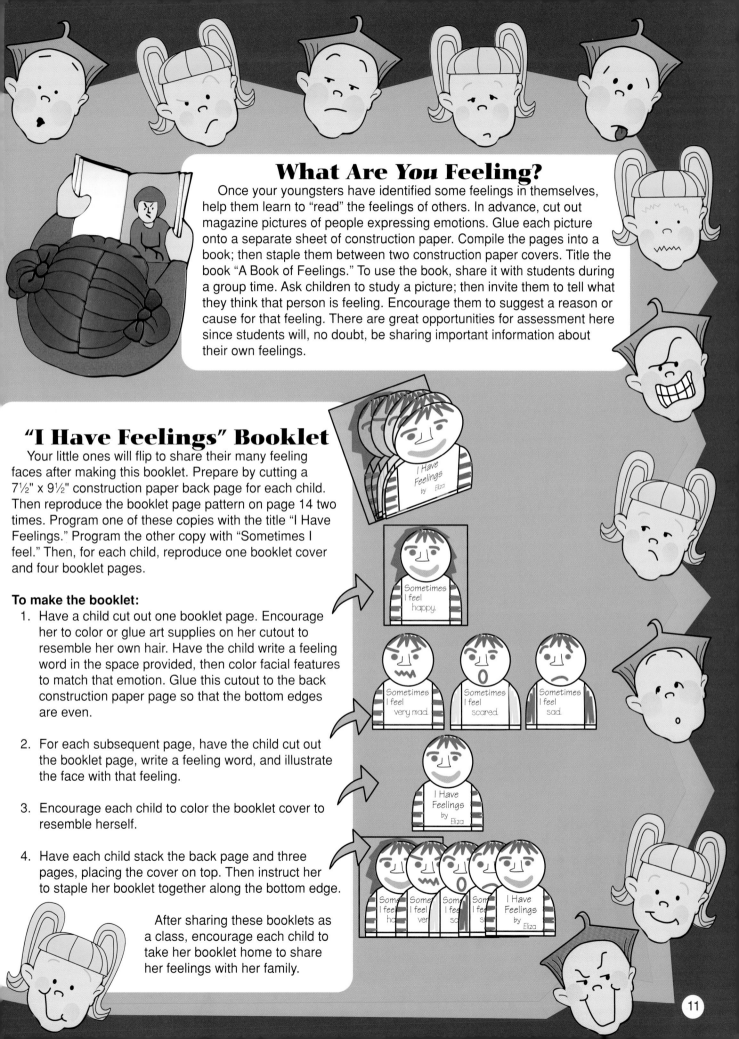

My Many Colored Days
Written by Dr. Seuss
Illustrated by Steve Johnson and Lou Fancher

Emotional truth blends with fun in this completely new and different kind of Dr. Seuss book. Beautiful, bubbling art accompanies the rich text that overflows with an array of emotions.

In advance, cut out a supply of construction paper strips in a variety of colors. Then share *My Many Colored Days*. After discussing the book, prompt youngsters to talk about what kinds of feelings certain colors bring about in themselves. Then link together the idea of colors representing moods by making mood chains. To begin invite each child in a small group to choose a few colored strips. Ask her to tell you how each color makes her feel; then write her response on the appropriate color strip. Have her glue her strips together to make a chain. Save each child's chain for use in the following activity.

Our Many Colored Days

Artistic expression is definitely allowed here! To prepare for this activity, cut out several child-shaped templates from tagboard. (Design your child patterns similarly to the ones shown in the illustration, with arms outstretched.) Stock your art easel with a supply of colorful paints and art paper. Arrange the child tracers, a tape recorder, and a collection of instrumental music nearby. Invite a child to listen to music as he paints a large sheet of paper to represent how the music makes him feel. As he uses different colors, prompt him to explain his choices of colors. When his painting is dry, direct the child to trace a child template onto his painting and then cut it out. Tape each child's mood chain (from the activity above) to one hand of his cutout. Tape the cutouts and mood chains together as shown. Hang the completed project across the ceiling of your classroom with a sign titled "Our Many Colored Days."

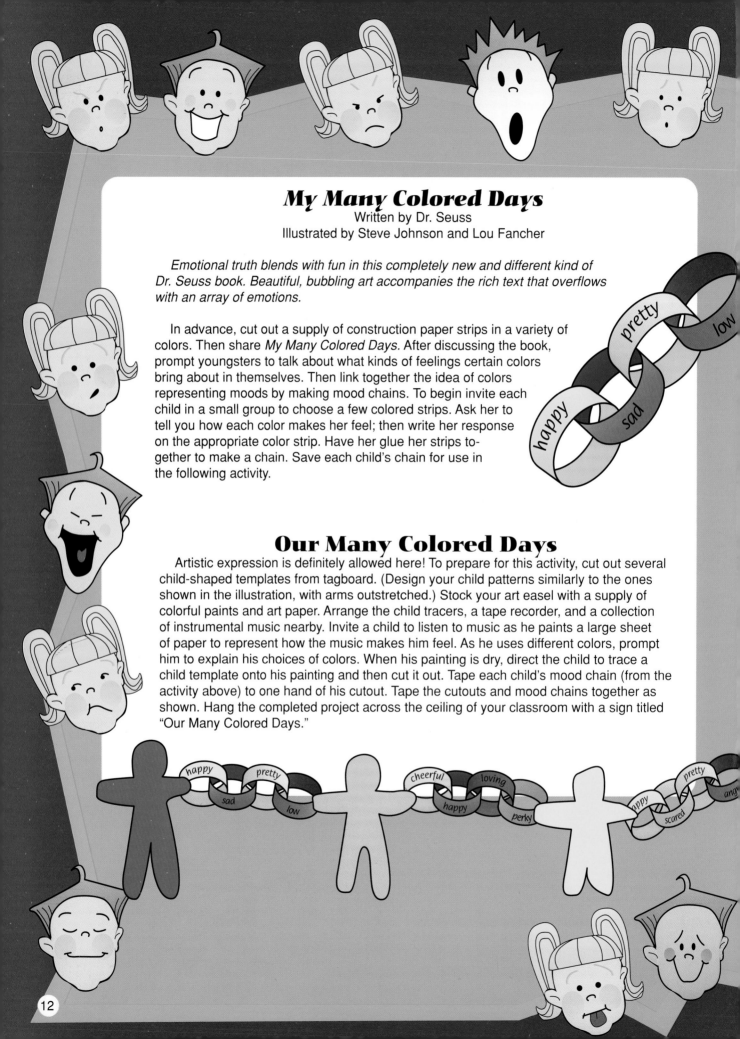

Feelings Box

Is it possible to hold a feeling in your hands? Well, not really, but you can come pretty close! Make a Feelings Box by separately covering a box and its lid with bulletin board paper. Then embellish the box with smiley-face stickers. Send home a note asking each parent to help his child find an item no bigger than a lunch bag that reminds him of a feeling. For example, a stuffed animal might remind a child of feeling safe, or a picture of a child on his soccer team may remind him of feeling proud. As each child brings in an item, have him place it in the Feelings Box. During group time, encourage each child to tell the group about the item and the feeling it brings him.

Feelings Memory

This memory game will give youngsters a picture-perfect opportunity to express a variety of feelings. Take a photo of each child dramatizing a particular feeling, such as mad, silly, happy, friendly, etc. Have double prints made of the film. Glue each picture onto an index card; then label it with the depicted feeling. Laminate the cards for durability. Spread the cards facedown on a playing area.

To play, invite each player, in turn, to turn over two cards. If the cards match, ask him to name the depicted feeling and then keep the cards. If the cards do not match, have the child turn them facedown again. Continue play until all the pairs have been matched.

Booklet Page Pattern
Use with "'I Have Feelings' Booklet" on page 11.

Building Character

*B*ecause you know that young children are concrete learners, do you sometimes experience difficulty teaching them abstract concepts such as fairness, honesty, and respect? The ideas in this section are designed to help you bring specific virtues into the experiential and observable realms of your little ones.

Helpfulness

Start the Wheels Turning

Inspire your students to start thinking about helpfulness by encouraging them to become aware of what others might need instead of focusing solely on their own needs. To begin this thinking process, share *Farmer Duck* by Martin Waddell. As you read aloud, stop on the page where the duck is "sleepy and weepy and tired." Encourage youngsters to discuss the story so far. Ask how they think the duck is feeling. Find out what they think might be helpful in that situation. Then have each child write about and illustrate his helpful idea. Encourage each child to share his page with the group; then finish reading the story aloud.

It's a Good Deal!

After introducing and discussing the idea of helpfulness, encourage children to share how they feel after they have helped someone. To stimulate discussion, if necessary, ask different children to help you right then. (For example, you might ask a child to bring you your chair or carry something to you. Then ask that child how she feels afterward.) Prompt children to recognize that in helping others, we often get a good feeling ourselves.

The farmer should get up!
Patrick

I would help the duck with his chores because I'm strong.
Kim

CHARACTER

Be on the Lookout

Explain to your youngsters that to help a friend or family member, one must be on the lookout for what others need. To help your little ones begin to recognize opportunities for helping, encourage them to share ways that they think they have been helpful at home, at school, or at play. Record their responses on chart paper. Encourage children to share new helping ideas as they occur in their lives. Add the new ideas to the list, as your youngsters are constantly on the lookout!

Help pick up trash.

Help wash the dog.

Put away toys.

Clean my room.

Help, I Need Somebody!

Youngsters will get a kick out of this cooperative challenge, and they'll enjoy giving and receiving all the help they possibly can! Divide your class into two lines. Give the leader of each line a Ping-Pong ball and a large spoon. Have the leaders balance their balls on their spoons while walking to a finish line and then back again. If one of them drops his ball, the other child must pick it up for him—all the while still holding his own spoon and ball—before walking on. This game just gets sillier and sillier, but all the giggles will teach youngsters that helping really is fun!

Honesty

ideas by Marie Iannetti and Lori Kent

Honesty Is the Best Policy

Since the concept of honesty may be vague for some young students, start this unit by asking your youngsters to explain what they think it means to be honest. Then follow up your discussion by sharing the story of George Washington and the cherry tree. Read this story, as found in *The Children's Book of Virtues* edited by William J. Bennett, or retell the story in your own words. Afterward, discuss with your students the outcome of the story: how George and his father felt after George told the truth. Encourage volunteers to share times when they were honest. Write their comments on a bulletin board paper cherry cutout. Display the cutout near the display described below.

I found a dime and gave it to Ms. Kent.
Nicholis

I told Mom when I broke a dish.
Donna

I told Ms. Murray that I was the one who was too noisy in the hall.
Brian

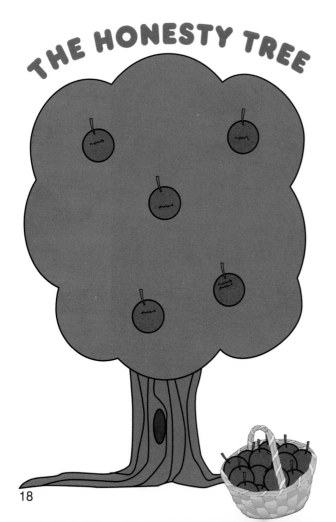

THE HONESTY TREE

Fruits of Honesty

Make this class display as a follow-up to the story of George Washington and the cherry tree. Cut out a large tree shape from bulletin board paper; then mount it on a wall or bulletin board. Title the display "The Honesty Tree." Next, cut out a large supply of construction paper cherry shapes. Store the cherries in a basket near the tree. Each time a child displays the trait of honesty, write the child's act on a cherry cutout. Invite that child to tell the class about his act of honesty; then have him tape the cherry to the tree. When the tree has the desired number of cherries on it, celebrate the fruits of honesty with an extended recess or another special privilege.

Virtues in the Classroom

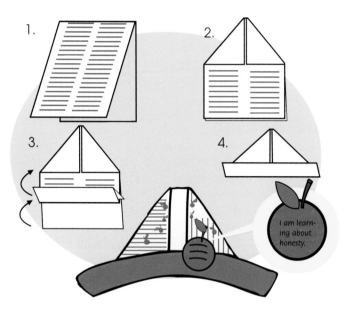

Honesty Hat

Remembering to be honest will always be foremost on your little ones' minds when they wear these hats. In advance, fold a newspaper hat for each child, following the illustrations shown. Also program one cherry cutout as shown for each child. Set out several trays of red paint and some sponge circles. Encourage each child to sponge-paint red circles on the triangular part of his hat. When the paint is dry, have him use markers to draw stems and leaves on the painted circles to resemble cherries. Finally, have him glue green construction paper trim across the brim of the hat. Top it all off by directing him to glue his programmed cherry to the brim of his hat. Now that's a cool hat, and that's the truth!

I-Cannot-Tell-a-Lie Pie

Invite your little truth-tellers to make this delicious pie. To make one, have a child place a graham cracker in a resealable plastic bag and crush it into crumbs. Direct him to pour the crumbs into an individual muffin-cup liner. Next, have him spoon vanilla pudding on top of the crumbs. Finally, instruct him to place a spoonful of prepared cherry pie filling on top of the pudding. Mmm…what a sweet reminder that honesty is the best policy!

A Truthful Tune

Reinforce the meaning of *honesty* by having your little ones clap, snap, or slap to the beat as they sing the following song.

(sung to the tune of "Row, Row, Row Your Boat")

Tell, tell, tell the truth.
Tell it every day,
'Cause if you do, it's good for you.
Honesty's the way!

Compassion, helpfulness, patience, respect, responsibility—the list of valuable, character-building qualities goes on and on, and so does the challenge of teaching these virtues to youngsters! Refer to these ideas for some practical, creative, and age-appropriate activities to use in the instruction, reinforcement, and rewarding of important life values in your students.

Cooperation

A Sticky Situation

If your efforts to have students cooperate with one another seem to come easily unglued, try this self-sticking activity. Group your youngsters into pairs. Ask each child to "glue" his elbow to his partner's elbow by interlocking them. Encourage the partners to keep their elbows attached while attempting to perform a task such as bouncing a ball across the room. After students have had time to experience success (or frustration) with the task, have them discuss the ways they tried to succeed. Summarize that in order to accomplish the task, each student had to work cooperatively with his partner. Then invite student pairs to "glue" another part of their bodies together, such as their knees, and try to perform other suggested tasks. By sticking with their partners, students can learn a lot about cooperation!

The Cooperation Web

Weave some cooperative skills among your students with this web-building activity. Have students stand in a circle. Explain that they will work together to build a web using a ball of yarn. Then, holding the loose end of the yarn with one hand, call out a student's name and toss the yarn ball to him. Encourage him to follow suit, being sure to grip the stretched piece of yarn with one hand as he tosses the ball of yarn with his other hand. Continue in this manner until all of the children are holding a section of the yarn so that it resembles a spider's web. Have the last child toss the ball of yarn back to you. After pointing out the results of everyone's cooperative efforts—a magnificent web—call on one child at a time to release the yarn. As the web collapses little by little, emphasize the importance of each child's role in building and supporting the web. What amazing things we can achieve when our efforts together we all weave!

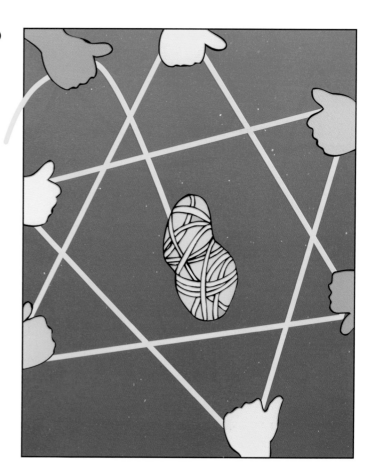

Lorri Ann Wahlgren, Point Pleasant, NJ

A Rainbow of Friends

Liken friendship to a rainbow—the combination of different colors creates a beautiful sight, just as the combination of different people can create wonderful friendships. Then invite children to create a rainbow. Set out red, yellow, and blue tempera paints. As a class, combine colors to create new colors until each color of the rainbow is represented. Have small groups each use a different color to sponge-paint a segment of a rainbow drawn on bulletin board paper. (If desired, designate the color to be painted in each segment.) Afterward, have each child create a self-portrait, paying careful attention to his color of hair, eyes, skin, etc. Display the rainbow with the title "A Rainbow of Friends." Then mount the self-portraits around the rainbow.

Susan Rushing—Gr. K, Metro Kids Care, Des Moines, IA

Photogenic Friendships

Capture those precious moments of friendship on film! Keep a camera in your classroom at all times; then take pictures of children as they spontaneously display qualities of friendship. Have the film developed in multiple prints; then mount a photo on a sheet of paper for each pictured child. Write that child's dictated statement about how or why the other pictured child (or children) is a friend. Encourage each child to take his friendship photo home to share. Both the student and his family will be pleased with the photogenic friendships that develop!

Gay Taylor—PreK, West Point Elementary, LaGrange, GA

My friend Alan helps me.
Devin

Hugs to Give, Hugs to Get

Have you given and received your quota of hugs today? Discuss that hugging a friend is one way to show you care. Have students say the rhyme below as they pass hugs to one another. Then invite youngsters to make this huggable project. Enlarge the hug pattern shown and make a class supply on construction paper. Have each child decorate the head section to resemble himself. Then encourage students to show their friendship by giving hugs to—and receiving hugs from—one another. As a child receives a hug, have him request the hugger's signature on his pattern. Then show students how to fold the arms on their patterns so that they appear to be giving hugs.

I have a hug. I give it to you.
Now you have a hug to give away too!

Fairness

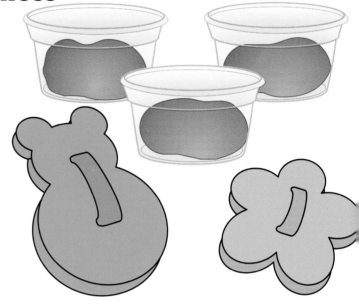

What's Fair?

Here's a neat way to call attention to the concept of fairness while introducing a mess of fraction fun. Read aloud Stuart Murphy's *Give Me Half!;* then help youngsters explore their ideas about ways the characters could (or whether they should) fairly share each item. Invite students to point out the fair and unfair attitudes/behaviors of each character. Then divide the class into student pairs. Give each pair an item or set of items that can be divided evenly between the partners—such as play dough or a set of blocks. Encourage each pair to decide how to use and share the materials in a fair manner. Will they each take half? Are there other ways to fairly share? Whatever the agreed-upon solution, it's what's fair for that pair.

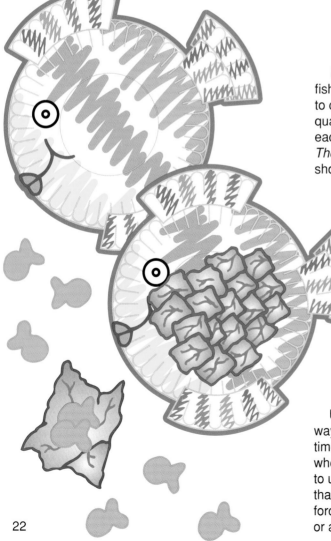

Balancing the Scales

Demonstrate how to balance the scales of cooperation with this fishy activity. In advance, use a paper plate and paper plate scraps to create a fish-shaped dish. To make fish scales, cut out a class quantity of foil squares, plus several extras. Wrap two edible fish in each foil square. Hide the scales around the room; then read aloud *The Rainbow Fish* by Marcus Pfister. After discussing the story, show students the fish dish, explaining that all the fish's scales have been lost. Ask students to search the room for the scales, placing those they find in the dish. Afterward, congratulate students for their shared search efforts. Next, explain that there is a little treat inside each of the scales. Ask students to discuss how the scales could be shared fairly. When everyone has agreed upon a fair method, distribute the scales accordingly. Cheers to our fair share!

adapted from an idea by Gayle Simoneaux and
    Ellen Knight—Gr. K
Pineville Park Weekday Early Education, Pineville, LA

We're All in This Together

Use this idea to help youngsters realize that fairness is not always measured in concrete terms. Just before beginning a cleanup time, signal students to stop their activity. Ask youngsters to discuss whether, and why, every student should help clean up. Guide them to understand that since they all used the materials, it is only fair that they all help clean up. Then invite the class to clean up, reinforcing each child's efforts with a compliment, a smile, a quick hug, or a sticker. Fair praise for everyone!

rtues in the Classroom

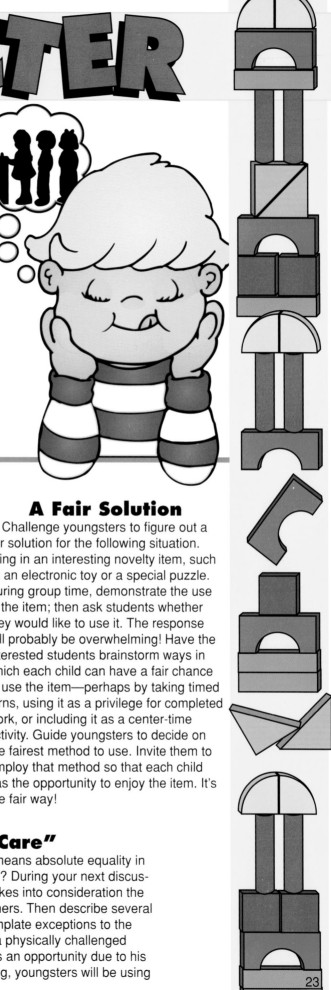

One Fair Turn Deserves Another

Explain to your class that rules, such as taking turns, are needed so that everyone is treated fairly. To illustrate your point, have youngsters close their eyes. Then ask each child to imagine that he is very thirsty and needs a drink of water. But when he reaches the water fountain, other students are already crowded around it. In fact, the crowding prevents any of the children from getting water. Ask children whether they think this is fair. Prompt students to share their solutions to the problem. Most likely the predominant response will involve taking turns. Capitalize on this opportunity to emphasize that taking turns—at the water fountain, at the slide, in the lunch line, to play a game, or even to get an adult's attention—is a tried-and-true way to ensure fairness to all.

A Fair Solution

Challenge youngsters to figure out a fair solution for the following situation. Bring in an interesting novelty item, such as an electronic toy or a special puzzle. During group time, demonstrate the use of the item; then ask students whether they would like to use it. The response will probably be overwhelming! Have the interested students brainstorm ways in which each child can have a fair chance to use the item—perhaps by taking timed turns, using it as a privilege for completed work, or including it as a center-time activity. Guide youngsters to decide on the fairest method to use. Invite them to employ that method so that each child has the opportunity to enjoy the item. It's the fair way!

Fair Means "Care"

Does your class believe that fairness means absolute equality in all things—time, quantity, and opportunity? During your next discussion on fairness, explain that being fair takes into consideration the feelings, needs, and circumstances of others. Then describe several situations to prompt youngsters to contemplate exceptions to the equality attitude—situations that involve a physically challenged child, a child who is ill, or one who misses an opportunity due to his involvement in a special class. Before long, youngsters will be using care when it comes to being fair.

23

Patience

Patience—it's a character trait that takes time to develop, especially in children! But with your patience and the ideas in this unit, your youngsters will soon become experts at practicing patience.

by Mackie Rhodes

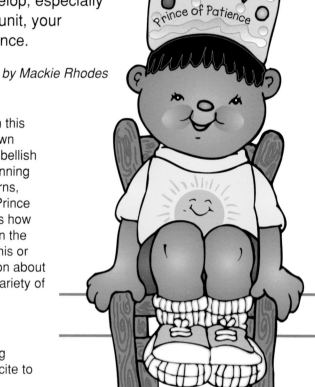

Regal Rewards

Recognize youngsters for their efforts at practicing patience with this regal idea. In advance, create two tagboard crowns. Label one crown "Prince of Patience" and the other "Princess of Patience." Then embellish each crown with an assortment of sparkling craft items. At the beginning of an activity during which students typically struggle with taking turns, ask for a volunteer to take the last turn. Then crown that child the Prince or Princess of Patience. Explain that this child will show classmates how to practice patience while waiting his or her turn. Have the child don the appropriate crown; then proceed with the activity until it is time for his or her turn. Afterward (or during a group time), guide a short discussion about the Prince's or Princess's experience. Repeat this process with a variety of appropriate classroom activities.

A Cheery Chant

As you know oh, so well, student patience is often needed during turn-taking activities. Teach youngsters this cheery little chant to recite to themselves to encourage patience during waiting times.

> I'm waiting as patient as can be
> For my turn to come to me.
> I'm waiting as patient as can be.
> I'm so very proud of me!

Patient Puppies

Now that students have been initiated into the art of being patient, make these special puppets to use as reminders to practice patience on a regular basis. To make the puppets, make several copies of the puppy patterns (page 26) on construction paper. Color and laminate each pup; then glue a large craft stick to the back. Put these puppies in a can labeled "Patient Puppies." Then explain to students that whenever they need a little patience booster while waiting for an activity or adult attention, they may take a puppy from the canister. The puppy serves as a reminder to the child to continue practicing patience. It also serves as a signal to others that the child is trying to be patient and as a cue to you to praise her for her efforts. When the child no longer needs the puppy, have her return it to the canister for the next child who might need a boost of patience.

irtues in the Classroom

"Paws" for Patience

While youngsters need to practice patience during turn-taking times, they also need to learn patience when they're engaged in daily activities. (Don't we all?) Use these special tickets with students who might be feeling frustrated or just need a short break from challenging activities. To prepare, make a supply of the tickets (page 26) on construction paper. Then cut out and laminate the patterns. As you monitor students during their various activities, offer patient "paws" tickets to youngsters who might need to take brief pauses from their activities. When a child receives a ticket, you might invite her to read a book to herself, walk once around the classroom, or just rest for a few minutes. Then have her return the ticket to you and return to her activity. Sometimes just a little "paws" will do!

Patience Puffs

Some activities and events, such as long assemblies or bus rides, can naturally induce a touch of impatience in students. When you can anticipate such an event, use this idea to puff a little patience into your youngsters. In advance, obtain a manual air pump that expels gentle puffs of air and label it "Patience Pump." During a group time, discuss the upcoming event with students. Then explain that you are going to help them wait patiently by giving them special puffs of patience. Show youngsters the pump and tell them that the puffs of patience are in it. Then pump a puff of air onto each child, explaining that this should give him enough patience to last through the event.

I'm being patient!

Patience Power!

A student's day requires so much patience! Use these powerful rewards to recognize your youngsters for practicing patience on a daily basis. Simply make and cut out a supply of the rewards on page 27. If desired, add a bit of color to each reward. Then periodically catch one, a few, or even all of your students practicing patience. Praise each student for using the power of patience; then give him a reward to wear so that he can show off his patience power.

Puppy Patterns
Use with "Patient Puppies" on page 24.

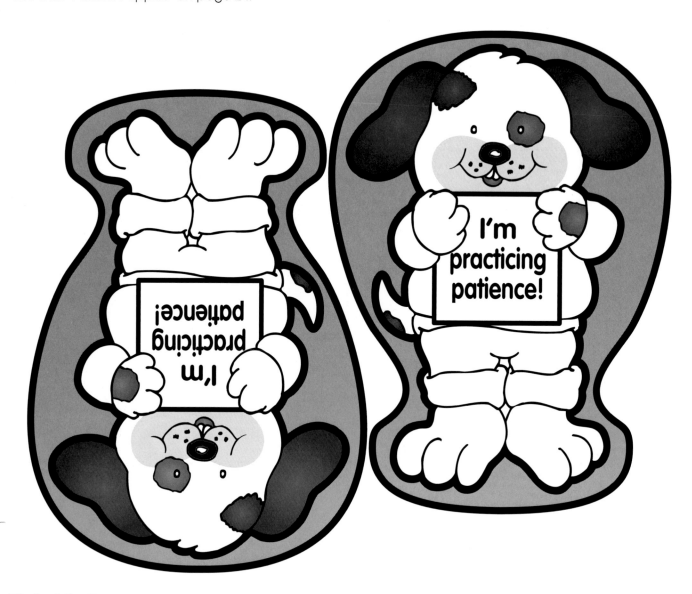

Ticket Patterns
Use with "'Paws' for Patience" on page 25.

"Paws" for Patience

"Paws" for Patience

"Paws" for Patience

©The Mailbox® • *Social Studies* • TEC60937

©The Mailbox® • *Social Studies* • TEC60937

©The Mailbox® • *Social Studies* • TEC60937

©The Mailbox® • *Social Studies* • TEC60937

Responsibility

Are your little ones anxious to take on jobs and duties in the classroom? Reach for these engaging activities to strengthen each child's sense of responsibility.

by Allison Ward

Count on Us

Start your unit with this lively language experience. In advance, label a different chart with one of each of the following headings: Home, School, Community. Engage students in a discussion about what responsibilities and jobs they have in each place. Write student responses on the charts and record how many children share a particular job (such as caring for a pet). Display the finished charts in your classroom under the title "Count on Us to Get the Job Done!"

Hey! I do that too!

Community

- I throw trash away. 18
- I look before crossing the street. 18
- I recycle. 9

Lend a Helping Hand

Line leader	Ryan
Door holder	Sarah
Gofer	Cory
Lunch helper	Ben
Trash collector	Rosa
Caboose	Katy

Lend a Helping Hand

Use this chart to remind each child when it's her turn to lend a hand with the classroom responsibilities. With your class, brainstorm a list of student jobs (such as line leader and door holder). List the jobs on a chart. Then attach a small hook side piece of Velcro fastener beside each job title. Next, give each child a piece of colorful construction paper. Direct the student to trace and cut out her handprint and then write her name across the palm. Laminate all the cutouts and then attach a corresponding loop side Velcro piece to the back of each hand. Assign duties by attaching a different hand beside each job on your chart. When a child sees her name on the chart, she'll know exactly what she is responsible for. Rotate your helping hands each week so everyone has lots of chances to lend a hand!

Recipe for Responsibility

Help satisfy each child's craving for responsibility with this tasty idea. Make a class set of page 30 on sturdy paper; then send a copy home with each child. When the completed recipes are returned, select a different student's recipe each week to share with the class. Then place that recipe and the necessary supplies in your cooking center for youngsters to independently prepare the snack and eat it. Encourage students to ask the recipe's author for help if necessary. Mmm, responsibility tastes good!

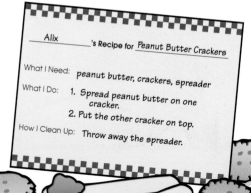

Alix's Recipe for *Peanut Butter Crackers*

What I Need: peanut butter, crackers, spreader

What I Do:
1. Spread peanut butter on one cracker.
2. Put the other cracker on top.

How I Clean Up: Throw away the spreader.

CHARACTER

Virtues in the Classroom

Responsibility Rhapsody

Tout this tune about taking on responsibility, replacing the third and fourth lines of the chorus with the appropriate verse lines. Your little ones will be belting it out in no time!

(sung to the tune of "If You're Happy and You Know It")

VERSE 1   If you need a job done well,
           Give a yell. (Yahoo!)
           If you need a job done well,
           Give a yell. (Yahoo!)

CHORUS   I'm responsible you see.
           You can depend on me.
           If you need a job done well,
           Give a yell. (Yahoo!)

VERSE 2   If you want it done on time,
           Watch for me. (Ticktock!)

VERSE 3   If you need a helping hand,
           I'll understand. (Oh, yeah!)

VERSE 4   If you want it done with pride,
           boys: I'm your guy! (*then girls:* I'm your girl!)

VERSE 3: Nod head.

VERSE 4: Wave hand.

VERSE 1: Raise arm over head.

VERSE 2: Tap wrist or wristwatch.

Dependable Reading

Once youngsters have identified and practiced being responsible, make a class book of their favorite duties. For each child, program a large sheet of construction paper with "I am responsible for _____. I like this job because _____." Have each child write or dictate to complete the sentence and then illustrate her page. Complete the book by binding all the pages behind a cover titled "You Can Depend on Me!" Place the finished book in your reading center for children to enjoy. Now that's some responsible reading!

Responsibility's Crowning Glory

Proclaim your students kings and queens of responsibility with these glowing crowns! First, give each child a manila tagboard sentence strip sized to fit his head. Encourage him to use the strip's guidelines to draw points of uniform depth across the top. Have him cut out the points and paint the crown yellow. Next, have him write his name in large letters with a glitter pen. When the glitter dries, provide craft glue and lots of shiny sequins, glitter, and plastic jewels so students can make their crowns sparkle! Once the entire crown dries, assist each child in stapling his crown together. Encourage little ones to wear their special crowns at school when they take on responsibility.

Parent Note and Recipe Card
Use with "Recipe for Responsibility" on page 28.

Dear Parent,

We've been cooking up ways to show responsibility in school! We need your help to create a cooking file in our classroom. On the card below, please help your child write his or her favorite "all-by-myself" recipe. (Simple snacks such as peanut butter crackers or a bowl of cereal are appropriate.) Please return the recipe by _____.

Each week one child's recipe will be selected and placed in the cooking center. Students will then prepare that recipe for snacktime. (Remember that it is important to choose a recipe that other children can create in our classroom and enjoy.) We are looking forward to tasting all the yummy recipes!

Thank you,

_____'s Recipe for _____

What I Need:

What I Do:

How I Clean Up:

Family

Families Are Fun!

We all know that families come in many different packages. In fact, no two are exactly the same! Introduce your students to the topic of families with these fun ideas.

by Sherri Lynn Kuntz and Angela VanBeveren

What is a family?
• people who love each other —Keisha
• A family is people you live with. —Brit
• They hug a lot. —Camille

Getting Started

Begin your family unit by having youngsters respond to the question "What is a family?" You are sure to get many different answers! Record each student's response on a sheet of chart paper. Then introduce some general information about families (see the facts below). Also record what students would like to learn about families. Display the chart for future reference and encourage students to add to it throughout the unit.

Families Are Special!

Use a familiar tune to get your youngsters in sync with families! During group time, sing the song below with your students. After the children know the song well, encourage them to come up with motions for each line. Are families special? Of course!

Families
(sung to the tune of "Ten Little Indians")

Some have fathers. Some have mothers.
Some have sisters. Some have brothers.
In some houses, there are others.
Every family's special!

Facts About Families

A family is made up of a group of people who live together.
Family members protect, nurture, teach, and provide for each other.
Sometimes family members look alike, and sometimes they do not.
Every person in a family helps make it special.
Families are alike in some ways and different in other ways.
Families can be large or small.
Other people sometimes live with a family.

Aren't They Great?

Show your students that families are bunches of fun with this listening activity. In advance, cut out a white poster board circle for each child. Instruct each student to use a permanent marker to draw a smiley face on her circle. Then have her use crayons to color the entire face. To complete the prop, have her tape a craft stick to the back of the face. Then gather your little ones and ask them questions such as "Does your family ever watch movies?" and "Does your family eat ice cream together?" Have students answer yes to questions by holding up their smiley-face props. Once youngsters get the idea, encourage them to take turns asking questions. Your youngsters will be all smiles as they realize that their families do many of the same fun things!

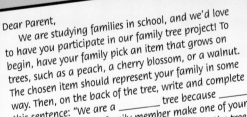

dad
mom
sister
brother
grandparents
aunts, uncles, and cousins
pets
yourself

Building a Family

Looking for a concrete way to examine the makeup of your students' families? Use Unifix cubes! In advance, program a piece of poster board with color-coded categories for each family member as shown. Then have each child pick an appropriate-colored cube to represent each family member living at her house, including herself and any pets. After she stacks the cubes, have the child say who each cube represents. Then ask questions such as "Who has the largest family?" and "Who has the most brothers?"

To create a more permanent representation of each family, have students make bracelets with beads corresponding to the colors in their stacks. Have each child string the beads onto a pipe cleaner in any order and then fill the remaining space with metallic beads. Now your little ones will be able to have family members with them all day long!

Dear Parent,
We are studying families in school, and we'd love to have you participate in our family tree project! To begin, have your family pick an item that grows on trees, such as a peach, a cherry blossom, or a walnut. The chosen item should represent your family in some way. Then, on the back of the tree, write and complete this sentence: "We are a _____ tree because _____." Have each family member make one of your chosen items (peach, blossom, etc.) to glue to the tree. You are encouraged to decorate your family tree using a variety of materials. Don't forget to put your family name on the front of the tree! Please return the project to school by ___Sept. 27___. Thanks for helping make school a fun place to be!

We are a peach tree because we are sweet.

Family Trees

Strengthen the home-school connection with this family tree project! In advance, make a tagboard copy of the pattern on page 35 for each child. Send the tree pattern home along with a note similar to the one shown. Encourage each child to help his family decorate the tree using a variety of materials. When the projects are returned to school, encourage each student to share his unique family tree with the rest of the class. As a finishing touch, display the family trees on a bulletin board. What a treat!

What Children Do Best

As we all know, every member of a family is important! This art activity will help each child understand his significance in his family. Read *What Mommies Do Best/What Daddies Do Best* by Laura Numeroff. After discussing the book, have students brainstorm other things that parents do. Record responses on a piece of chart paper. Then ask each child to think of one thing that he does best and have him draw a picture of the activity on a sheet of construction paper. Label students' drawings and then display them on a bulletin board with the title "What Children Do Best!" If desired, include a modified phrase similar to the one from the book's ending. What a masterpiece!

What Children Do Best!

Theo can feed the dog.

Alice can dust.

But best of all, children can give you lots and lots of love!

Alex can make his bed.

Jill can set the table.

School Families Are Sweet!

Culminate your family unit with this yummy circle game that extends the idea of a family to the classroom setting. Explain that classroom members are a special type of family. Review "Facts About Families" on page 32 and discuss how they relate to school. To play the game, chant the rhyme below with your students while passing around a piece of wrapped candy. When the rhyme has ended, have the student with the piece of candy share something positive about a school friend. Then have her give the candy to the child next to her and move to the middle of the circle. When all of your sweeties are in the middle, encourage a group hug. Then give each student a piece of candy to munch on. Now that's a wonderfully sweet ending!

We are sweet.
We are neat!
We are a family.
What a treat!

The _____

Family Tree

A Family Affair

Today's families come in all shapes and sizes. Though families of the present may appear to look different from those of the past, the purposes of families remain the same. Families teach, protect, nurture, love, and provide for their children. Use the following activities to explore your students' individual families.

ideas contributed by Lucia Kemp Henry

What Is a Family?

Just what is a family anyway? Pose that question to your students and write their responses on chart paper. Then read aloud "What Is a Family?" from Mary Ann Hoberman's *Fathers, Mothers, Sisters, Brothers: A Collection of Family Poems*. After discussing the poem, ask youngsters whether they would like to add anything to their original definitions, and write their responses on the chart paper. Guide youngsters in summarizing the list to come up with a student-generated definition of *family*.

Family Portraits

The best thing about these family portraits is that youngsters don't have to dress up, comb their hair, or keep their clothes clean for a single minute. The beauty of it all truly comes from the crayon of the beholder! Prepare a bulletin board by mounting a construction paper picture frame around the border. Then have each child think about who (and what) makes up his family. Give each child a large sheet of construction paper and crayons, paints, or other art materials. Have each child create a portrait of his family; then encourage him to write (or dictate) about his family. Provide time for each child to share his family portrait and creative writing during a group time. Encourage children to recognize the similarities and the unique traits among the families represented. Then mount each picture on the bulletin board.

Graphing Families

These graphs will help youngsters recognize the similarities and differences among their families. Make a graph for each family concept that you'd like to study. For example, you could make a graph for the number of people in a family, the number of children in a family, or the number of pets in a family. Photocopy each child's school photo several times. Have each child represent herself on each graph by mounting her photo in the appropriate column. As you summarize the graphs, be sure to give value to all of the families represented.

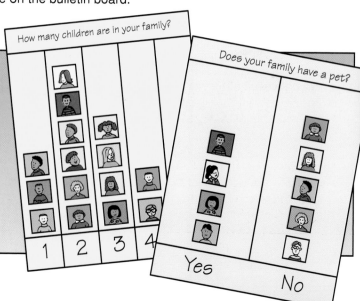

Family Traditions

While five- and six-year-olds may not be aware of their specific family traditions, this activity will help each child become aware of and appreciate her family traditions and the traditions of other families. Stimulate a discussion on family traditions by asking questions such as "What does your family do on weekends?", "How does your family celebrate birthdays?", and "What is your family's favorite food?" Help each child identify her family's tradition; then have her illustrate and write about the tradition. Post the finished projects on a bulletin board entitled "Tradition, Tradition!"

On Saturdays, me and my dad play soccer.

When there are shooting stars, my dad wakes me up to see.

Callie

Family Show-and-Tell

Family show-and-tell provides a wonderful opportunity for each family to get to know you and your class and vice versa. Send a copy of the parent note (page 38) home with each student. Encourage families to come to school with as many family members as they can. If you have families that are from other cultures, be sure to have them share about those cultures with your children.

Dear Parent,

We are studying families in school, and we'd love to meet yours! Please sign up for one of the dates below and bring as many family members as you can. Be prepared to share with us something that is special to your family. You could share photographs, a favorite family recipe, a song, a game, a pet, etc. Be creative—we just want to get to know your family!
Thank you!

Ms. Henry

Sizing It Up

Explore each child's wishes regarding the size of family he thinks he would like to have. Record each child's wish. Then read aloud *Louanne Pig in the Perfect Family* by Nancy Carlson. In this story, Louanne has a family of three—but she thinks that George's family of ten is the perfect size for a family. Children will laugh as well as think when Louanne gets a chance to experience the grass on the other side of the backyard fence!

After sharing the story, encourage children to discuss the advantages and disadvantages of having a large or small family. Then ask each child whether he would like to change his family-size wish that you recorded earlier.

Our Classroom Family

Discuss with your youngsters the ways in which your class is like a family. Using the topic sentences below as discussion starters, encourage each child to share how each sentence applies to his family as well as your classroom family.

- We have lots of different people.
- We work and play together.
- We help each other.
- We care about each other's feelings.
- We disagree and compromise.

After your discussion, create a visual display of classroom unity. Reproduce a pattern from page 39 on construction paper for each child. Then ask each child to color his person to resemble himself. Cut out the people patterns; then mount them in a circle around the title "Our Classroom Family."

Our Classroom Family

Parent Note Patterns

Use with "Family Show-and-Tell" on page 37.

Dear Parent,

We are studying families in school, and we'd love to meet yours! Please sign up for one of the dates below and bring as many family members as you can. Be prepared to share with us something that is special to your family. You could share photographs, a favorite family recipe, a song, a game, a pet, etc. Be creative—we just want to get to know your family!

Thank you!

Dear Parent,

We are studying families in school, and we'd love to meet yours! Please sign up for one of the dates below and bring as many family members as you can. Be prepared to share with us something that is special to your family. You could share photographs, a favorite family recipe, a song, a game, a pet, etc. Be creative—we just want to get to know your family!

Thank you!

©The Mailbox® • *Social Studies* • TEC60937

An Event to Remember

Turn the spotlight on your students' grandparents and other older friends by planning a classroom celebration in their honor. Follow these simple steps to create an occasion that will be cherished and remembered by all!

Grand Invitations

Be sure to give plenty of notice to your anticipated guests of honor. As a class, discuss the important elements of an invitation; then create an invitation for your grandparent celebration. Make a class supply of the invitations and assist students as they fill out their personal copies. Or have students carefully copy and complete their invitations. Be sure to make special arrangements for students whose grandparents are unable to attend. These students may wish to invite other older relatives or friends.

Dear _Nana_,

You Are Invited to a Special Celebration!

When: *September 26 at 2 o'clock*

Where: *Jay's classroom*
Southgate School, Room 7
101 Robin Lane

I hope you can come!

Papa Joe

A Warm Welcome

In preparation for your grandparent celebration, have each child craft a nametag for his special visitor. Then, on the day of the event, have each child welcome his guest and present him with the personalized nametag. As students show their guests around the classroom, encourage them to spotlight the projects and decorations that were completed in their grandparents' honor.

Marvelous Memories

For a fun icebreaker, give each student a copy of page 42 and have her use the questions on the page to interview her guest. Each child and her guest may work together to record the guest's responses on the lines. Once the interviews are complete, ask each child to introduce her guest to the rest of the class. Suggest that a child state her guest's full name and share one or two facts about her guest that she learned during the interview. If desired, follow up each introduction by asking the guest to attach a sticky dot to a world map to show his or her place of birth. After the introductions have been completed, take time to talk about the different birthplaces shown on the map.

I'd like to introduce my grandma, Gracie Foster.

Perfect Partners

Keep the atmosphere of your celebration upbeat and relaxed by planning several partner activities for students and their guests to complete. If desired, briefly introduce each center activity; then assign each pair to a center. After the pairs have worked at their assigned centers for about 15 to 20 minutes, use a predetermined signal to rotate the pairs clockwise to the next center. Continue in this manner until each pair has visited every center. Suggestions for centers include the following:

- **Game Center:** A few days before the event, ask students to bring games from home for this center. Suggest games that can be played by partners or foursomes, like checkers, dominoes, card games, and easy-to-play board games.

- **Puzzle Center:** Feature one large or several small jigsaw puzzles at this center for students and their guests to assemble.

- **Mystery Word Center:** For this center, place construction paper squares labeled with the letters needed to spell "grandparent" in each of several resealable plastic bags. Also place at the center copies of a reproducible like the one shown. Each child and his guest work together to create as many words as possible using the letters in one resealable bag. Set aside time later in the celebration for the pairs to share the words they created.

- **Reading Center:** At this center, place a large basket of your students' favorite books. Each child chooses a story to read to or with his guest.

- **Writing Station:** Stock this center with story paper, pencils, and crayons. Each twosome thinks about some of the special times that they've shared. Then the pair chooses one special time to describe and illustrate on a sheet of story paper. Provide a place at the center for the pairs to leave their completed work. After everyone has completed the center, compile the papers into a class book.

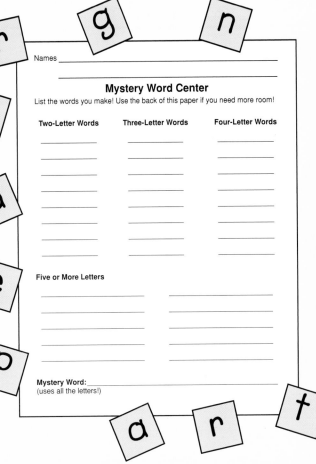

Names _____

Mystery Word Center

List the words you make! Use the back of this paper if you need more room!

Two-Letter Words	Three-Letter Words	Four-Letter Words
_____	_____	_____
_____	_____	_____
_____	_____	_____
_____	_____	_____
_____	_____	_____
_____	_____	_____
_____	_____	_____

Five or More Letters

_____   _____

_____   _____

_____   _____

_____   _____

Mystery Word: _____
(uses all the letters!)

A Grand Finale

As a culmination to the day, enlist your students' help in serving their guests a tasty snack of cookies and milk. While everyone is enjoying the snack, ask your guests to reminisce about their school days of long ago. No doubt your students will have a few questions for the guests as well. This would also be a good time for the pairs to share the words they made at the Mystery Word Center (see the description above). Then, last but not least, invite your guests to return to the classroom. Whether a grandparent is listening to students read, helping students practice math facts, or joining a young friend for lunch, these special visits will be looked forward to by all.

Name_____

Marvelous Memories

Ask your guest the following questions.
Write his or her answers on the lines.

1. What is your full name? _____

2. Where were you born? _____

3. In what year were you born?_____

4. What were your favorite toys as a child?_____

_____

5. What did your family like to do for entertainment?_____

_____

6. What is your favorite grade-school memory?_____

_____

7. What do you enjoy doing now?_____

_____

8. What is your favorite place in the whole world?_____

_____

9. What inventions have changed the way you live?_____

_____

10. What one thing do you wish had not changed over the years?

_____

_____

©The Mailbox® • *Social Studies* • TEC60937

42   **Note to the teacher:** Use with "Marvelous Memories" on page 40.

Homes

There's No Place Like Home

A Collection of Books About Houses and Homes

Nothing is quite as important to a child as home. And children's homes range from cozy and comfortable to lofty and luxurious. But homes aren't just for humans. There are homes for crabs, chimps, and crocodiles as well. In fact, the earth is filled with homes—and the earth is home to us all. Build a strong foundation for an understanding of shelter with these homey books about houses.

by Kim T. Griswell

A House Is a House for Me
Written by Mary Ann Hoberman
Illustrated by Betty Fraser

If it's time to start your youngsters thinking about houses and homes, then this is the book for you! Houses have never been so much fun!

Youngsters will love discovering what kind of house is a house for each class member with this special baggie book. Gather one plastic zippered bag for every two students. After sharing *A House Is a House for Me,* give each child a piece of tagboard cut to fit inside a baggie. Ask him to draw a picture of his home and write his name. To make the baggie book, staple all the baggies together along the bottom of the bags. Put a strip of heavy tape over the staples to form the book's spine. Insert two finished pages back-to-back inside each baggie; then zip each bag closed. Place the finished book in your reading center for students to page through and enjoy.

How a House Is Built
Written and Illustrated by Gail Gibbons

Using the language of building and simple art, Gibbons shows youngsters how a house is built. The step-by-step instructions provide a blueprint for understanding the contribution of each person who helps build the house.

Nail down your students' knowledge about tools as you build their reading skills and vocabularies. Ahead of time, collect house-building tools such as a hammer, screwdriver, level, and paintbrush. Write the name of each tool on a separate sentence strip. (As an alternative, copy and cut apart the tool pictures and labels on page 47.) Add a color dot to code each tool and a matching color dot on the back of each corresponding sentence strip. Then fill a handyman's apron with the tools and share *How a House Is Built.* Afterward, pull out each tool from your apron in turn. Ask a volunteer to name the tool and briefly describe how it is used. Then spread the tools and the labels along a table. Challenge students to try to decode each label and then match it to the corresponding tool. Advise them to check the color dots to see whether they've matched each item correctly. That's a match!

A Very Special House
Written by Ruth Krauss
Illustrated by Maurice Sendak

A book that begins with the line "dee dee dee oh-h-h" has to be fun. Sendak's childlike drawings combine with Krauss's skip-dee-doo language to create a one-of-a-kind house perfect for any child with imagination.

After reading this book, try this phonics rhyming exercise. Ahead of time make two flip charts: one with beginning consonants and another with sounds based on the book, such as "ee," "iddle," and "ooie." Stand the two charts side by side. Instruct children to begin by saying the word formed when you read the two charts together. Then flip each consonant, in turn, to reveal the next word. Youngsters will read each resulting word three times in chorus (for example, "Dee, dee, dee; bee, bee, bee"). After children have read through all the consonants for each phrase, encourage them to shout, "More, more, more!" Flip to the next sound on your chart and continue as before.

This House Is Made of Mud
Written by Ken Buchanan
Illustrated by Libba Tracy

In a house made of mud, nature is as close as a breeze through an open window. Delicate watercolors enliven a look at a family living in its desert home. Spanish text is offered alongside English.

In advance, have each child bring in a rinsed, lunch-size milk carton. Cut off the top as shown. For each group of six children, obtain a two-gallon bucket, two quarts of clay-like soil, one quart of sand, and one-eighth quart of straw (cut in two-inch pieces). After sharing the book, invite students to help mix the soil, sand, and straw in the bucket, adding enough water to create a workable, doughlike consistency. Then have each child pack enough of the mixture into his carton to fill it two-thirds full. When the brick is set, have him tip his brick out of the carton. Place the bricks in a warm, sunny location. Turn them often until they are uniform in color. When the bricks have dried, set up an adobe-brick center for house-building fun!

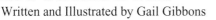

The House on East 88th Street
Written and Illustrated by Bernard Waber

There are strange sounds coming from the house on East 88th Street. What could it be? There's never a dull moment in the Primms' new home with this noisy guest.

Invite creative thinking with noise, noise, and more noise. In advance, record one common household noise in each room of a house, such as the shower spraying in the bathroom or the dishwasher running in the kitchen. For each room, speak the name of the room into the microphone; then record the sound. On legal-size paper, draw an outline of your house and label each room. Make a class supply. After reading the book, hand out the copies. Play the recorded noise for each room in turn. Point to the room on your outline. In the corresponding room on her outline, have each student draw what creature she imagines might be making the noise. Display the finished imaginings for students to compare.

The Salamander Room
Written by Anne Mazer
Illustrated by Steve Johnson

A young boy's room is transformed into the perfect home for a salamander. Lush illustrations combine with the text in this book to show the way homes (or habitats) fit the needs of the animals that live in them.

Transform the way your students think about bringing pets into their homes. Share and discuss *The Salamander Room;* then give each student a large sheet of paper. Have him draw a picture of his room. Then encourage him to choose an unusual pet and imagine the changes he would need to make in his room to make the pet feel at home. Have him add the changes to his drawing. Have each student, in turn, share his drawing with the class and describe the changes he made for his pet.

The Napping House
Written by Audrey Wood
Illustrated by Don Wood

This sleepy cumulative tale heaps on the fun as a snoring granny, a dreaming child, a dozing dog, a snoozing cat, and a slumbering mouse pile atop a cozy bed. When a flea bites the mouse, mayhem erupts. This is a gleeful book about naptime in a very colorful house.

How many students can fit in a bed? Your youngsters will hop into bed without arguing when you challenge them to find out. Ahead of time, tape a large bed outline on the floor in an open area. Have students form a large circle around the bed. Tell students that you will play a tape. When the music begins, they must hop toward the outline and into bed. When you stop the music, they must stop. Each time you stop the music, ask a different student to count those inside the outline. Write down the number on the board. Ask those in the bed to step out; then start the music again. After the game ends, look at the numbers on the board to discover the greatest number of students that hopped into the bed.

A House for Hickory
Written by Kelly Mazzone
Illustrated by Pat Reynolds

With suitcase in hand, Hickory the mouse sets out to find himself a house. But all of the houses Hickory discovers are occupied…until he finds the perfect house for a mouse. Your youngsters will love lifting the flaps to reveal who lives in each house Hickory finds.

After enjoying Hickory's journey, add to the fun with this poem.

Where can a mouse
find a house?

In a shiny shell?
No, a snail lives there.

In a woven basket?
No, a cat lives there.

In a golden hive?
No, bees live there.

In a neat straw nest?
No, birds live there.

In a deep, dark hole?
No, a rabbit lives there.

Where can a mouse
find a house?

In a snug, soft slipper?
Yes!

hammer	
screwdriver	
level	
paintbrush	
shovel	
saw	
tape measure	

Right at Home

Explore homes with these ideas, which introduce students to what almost all homes have in common—a foundation, a frame, running water, and electricity!

by Donna Battista

It's All About Blueprints

It takes planning to build a house. Help your students understand this by sharing real blueprints with them. In advance, ask a local builder for several old or discarded blueprints. Explain to students that the prints are created to show a builder how a house is to be constructed. The prints show how large the rooms will be and where the plumbing and electrical outlets and wiring will be located. Demonstrate how to draw a blueprint of your classroom by using a piece of white chalk to sketch its layout on a 12" x 18" sheet of blue construction paper. Then provide each youngster with a sheet of blue construction paper and a piece of chalk. Have him draw a blueprint of his room at home, including the location of electrical fixtures. What great planning!

A Home—The Inside Story

This virtual tour is sure to give students an inside look at a home's construction. Make arrangements with a local contractor to videotape a home construction site. Have the contractor explain the various components of the structure, such as the foundation, frame, plumbing pipes, electrical wiring, and general layout of the home. If possible, videotape the construction site at different stages to show the home's progress. Invite the contractor to visit your classroom. During the visit, share the virtual tour of the construction site with students. After viewing the video, encourage students to discuss what they have seen and ask any questions of your guest. Now that's constructive learning!

Showing Support

Use this idea to demonstrate how the frame of a house supports the structure. Display a folded card table and discuss how the table is supported when in use. Lead students to discuss the number of legs needed to hold up the table. Then pull up one leg at a time and test the sturdiness of the table. After all legs have been extended, stand the table upright. Explain to youngsters that the legs of the table create a frame that supports it, just as the frame of a house supports its walls and roof. Then provide each student with several small gumdrops or mini marshmallows and several wooden coffee stirrers. Encourage her to use the materials to create a freestanding frame. Have each child share her frame with the class. If desired, provide gumdrops or marshmallows for a class snack. What a tasty structure!

Putting It All Together

Who knew that a trip to the sink could create so much learning! Have students take a look under your classroom sink. Discuss with students the purpose of the pipes, leading them to understand that some pipes bring clean water into the sink and one takes dirty water away. Then create some hands-on play by adding several PVC pipes and joints to your water table. Have youngsters construct pipes with bends and then test out their handiwork with water. What wet fun!

My Home

This clever booklet will wrap up your mini home unit and remind students of several house components. Gather the materials listed below and then guide each youngster through the directions to complete his home booklet. Encourage each child to take his booklet home and share it with his family.

Materials for one booklet:
copy of the booklet on pages 50, 51, and 52
1" x 7" piece of sandpaper (foundation)
several wooden coffee stirrers (frame)
crayons
9" x 12" sheet of construction paper cut into a house shape as shown
2" red construction paper heart
glue
scissors
access to a stapler

Directions:
All pages: Cut out each of the booklet pages
Cover: Color the cover.
          Write your name.
Page 1: Glue on the foundation.
Page 2: Glue on the frame.
Page 3: Make a blue X on each water source. Color the
          picture.
Page 4: Draw a yellow circle around each electrical item.
          Color the picture.
Page 5: Color the picture. Cut along the dotted lines.
Back cover: Stack the pages in order and staple them to the back cover.
              Glue a heart to the back cover so it shows through the cut door
              on the last page.

My Home
by Sam

My Home

by _____

©The Mailbox® • *Social Studies* • TEC60937

My home has a foundation.

1

My home has a frame.

2

My home has plumbing.

3

My home has electricity.

4

My home is filled with love!

5

Careers

When I Grow UP

by Lucia Kemp Henry

Take a fresh approach to career studies with these activities. A reproducible gameboard, student-made booklet, and reproducibles are designed to minimize your preparation time.

School Careers

Although they observe school personnel daily, students are frequently unaware of their job titles or exactly what they do. Take photographs of school staff, including the nurse, cook, janitor, secretary, bus driver, teacher's assistant, and principal. Post the photographs on a bulletin board. Under each photo, post a brief job description. (For example, you might write "I am the school nurse. I take care of sick children.") Then ask school personnel to speak to your students about their jobs and give tours of their workstations.

"I Can Work Outdoors" Booklet

Creating this booklet gives youngsters an opportunity to picture themselves in several outdoor-oriented careers. Prepare for the activity by duplicating pages 58–63 on white construction paper for each student. On pages 58–62, cut on the dotted lines with an X-acto knife. Staple each set of booklet pages between colorful covers. To the inside back cover of each booklet, attach a student's picture so that his face shows through the opening in each page. (If pictures are not available, each student may draw his face on the inside back cover of the booklet.)

Discuss each occupation and its environment before having students color the figure and background. Have students color and attach the corresponding pieces from page 63 to complete each scene. (Or provide a variety of magazine cutouts for students to use.)

Let's Go! Lotto

Focus on transportation-related careers with this lotto game. On tagboard, duplicate the vehicle cards and gameboard on page 57. Have each student cut out the cards and match them to the occupations represented on the gameboard. Then have students discuss other careers that are dependent on vehicles.

Career Chorus

To introduce service-oriented careers, have a sing-along! Sing these verses to the tune of "The Farmer in the Dell" and then have students create more verses.

A Job That's Right for You

Verse 1:
A farmer works his fields.
A farmer works his fields.
Hi, ho, the derry-o,
A farmer works his fields.

Chorus:
There are so many jobs
That you might want to do.
Take time and you will find
A job that's just right for you.

Verse 2:
A dentist cleans our teeth.
Repeat Chorus
Verse 3:
A teacher works at school.
Repeat Chorus
Verse 4:
A barber cuts our hair.
Repeat Chorus
Verse 5:
A waiter serves us food.
Repeat Chorus

Occupation Scrapbook

Give children a chance to learn about careers and to share their knowledge with others. Have students cut out magazine pictures of people at work. Discuss the clippings and determine the occupations associated with them. Compile the pictures in a class scrapbook and have students dictate sentences about each occupation. Store the scrapbook in your reading area and invite students to look at it during their spare time.

Career Kits

Gather props to encourage roleplaying of various careers. For postal workers, for example, you might borrow an old mailbag, a postal hat and jacket, a rubber stamp, and a zip code book. Paint a sturdy produce box red, white, and blue. Then fill it with junk mail, a cardboard sectional divider (for sorting mail) and the other props. Make several different career kits. Introduce them to the dramatic-play area one at a time.

Check Your Resources

Utilize the career-education resources that are available to you.

- Take field trips that will give students insights into career opportunities. Be sure to include visits to a local fire station, police department, hospital, grocery store, dentist's office, beauty salon, park, library, bank, mall, or farm.
- Show films about careers. Children especially love to see films that tell how things are made and about the people who make them.
- Invite guest speakers into your classroom. People with interesting hobbies or talents make great teachers—especially if they demonstrate their skills.
- Check out a variety of library books about careers. Begin with *What People Do* from the Let's Discover series.
- Begin discussions with study prints. Your school library or resource center may have a collection of study prints designed to stimulate discussions on careers.

"When I Grow Up" Bulletin Board

Have students illustrate the jobs they find most appealing. (Discuss a wide range of career options.) Then ask students to draw large pictures of themselves in the careers of their choice. (Or have students select and glue magazine pictures to construction paper.) As each child completes the statement "I want to be a …," write the sentence at the bottom of his picture. Post these portraits on a bulletin board with the poster on page 56.

When I Grow Up

by Lucia Kemp Henry

Someday soon
When I grow up,
I'll have a job to do.
I'll sew a coat
Or sail a boat
Or work inside a zoo.

I might want
To drive a bus
Or teach children to read.
I'll load a train
Or fly a plane
Or plant a little seed.

So many jobs
That I might choose.
I wonder what I'll be?
I'll work and learn
'Til it's my turn
To find a job for me!

Note to the teacher: Use with "'When I Grow Up' Bulletin Board" on page 55.

1

I am a farmer. I work on a farm.

2

I am a ranger. I work in a park.

3

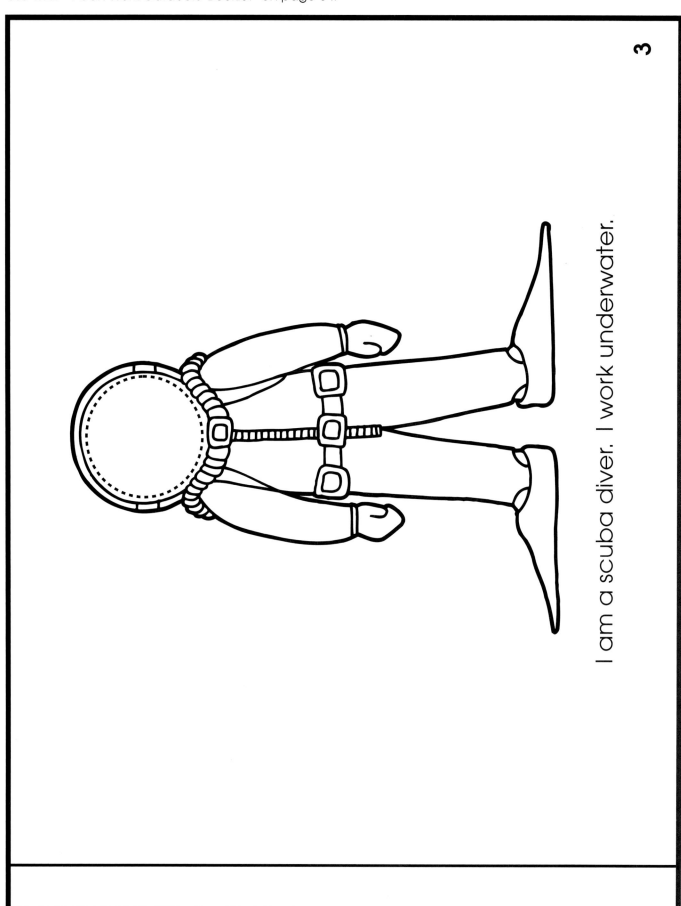

I am a scuba diver. I work underwater.

4

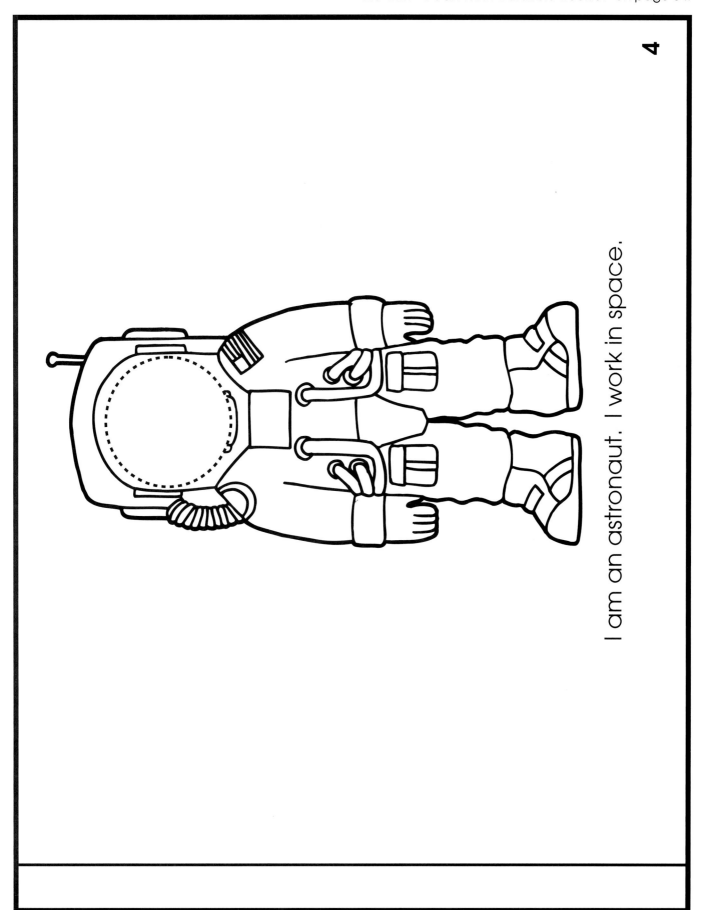

I am an astronaut. I work in space.

5

This is me. I am working outdoors.

Making Art

Do you like to make pretty pictures?

You can be an illustrator, a painter, or a photographer.

Cut and glue to make a picture.

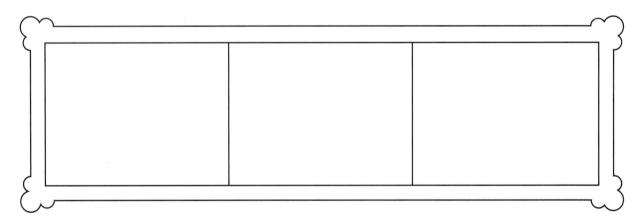

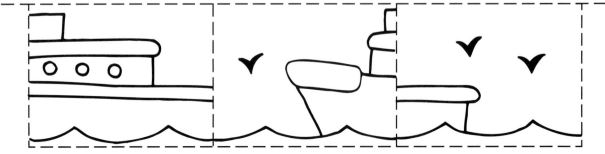

Helping

Do you like to care for dolls and pets?

You can be a doctor, a nurse, or a veterinarian.

 Color the picture.

Trace.

Some people like to

Imagining

Do you like to
make up stories?

You can be a writer,
a film director, or
an actor.

Color the things writers use.

©The Mailbox® • *Social Studies* • TEC60937

Driving

Do you like to play with trucks?
You can be a truck driver, a mechanic, or a factory worker.

Follow the dots.

Color.

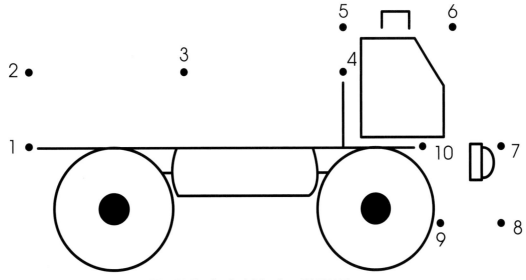

Building

Do you like to build
with blocks?

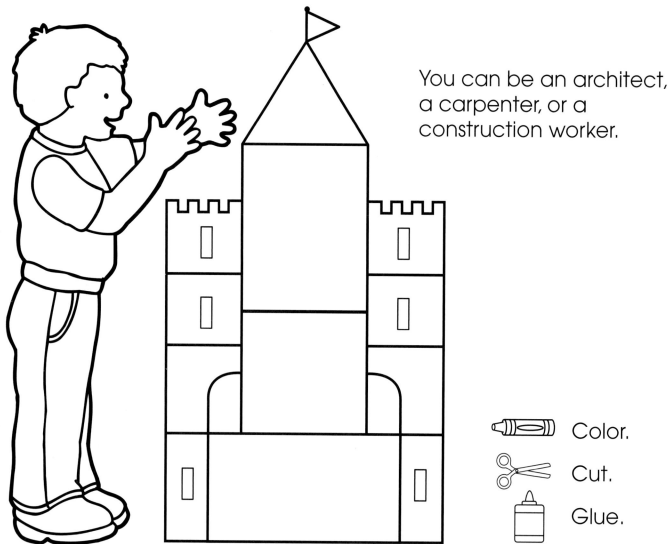

You can be an architect,
a carpenter, or a
construction worker.

Color.

Cut.

Glue.

Maps and Geography

Once Upon a Map...

Connect literature with social studies as you use traditional tales to introduce map skills to your students. Gather your favorite versions of the tales listed below; then use the extension ideas that follow to plot a course for a very happy ending—new knowledge about maps!

ideas by Randi Austin, Susan Bunyan, and Rachel Castro

Tales to Be Mapped Out

The Tortoise and the Hare
The Town Mouse and the Country Mouse
The Gingerbread Man
The Three Bears
Little Red Riding Hood
Cinderella
Jack and the Beanstalk

The Race Route

Use that "wascally wabbit" and the wise tortoise to introduce your little ones to map symbols. To prepare, create a map showing a possible route for the race, similar to the one shown. Make sure to include a road, a tree, a river, and a picnic table. Then copy, color, and cut apart the cards on pages 73 and 74. Shuffle the cards and set them aside.

After sharing a version of the tale, show youngsters your map. Have a volunteer use his finger to trace the route from start to finish. Then explain each of the symbols from the map key and have a different volunteer find an example on the map.

Extend this idea further with this fun movement game. Create motions for each of the four symbols depicted on the cards that students will perform when they see each card. For example, have students run in place when they see the road, pretend to sleep when they see the tree, pretend to swim when they see the river, and pretend to eat when they see the picnic table. Start showing the set of cards one by one and invite the children to perform the corresponding motion. For added fun, have them perform the motions slowly like a tortoise or quickly like a hare. Everyone's a winner here!

City Map, Country Map

Your youngsters will enjoy creating their very own three-dimensional map in this idea. After reading *The Town Mouse and the Country Mouse,* use a black permanent marker or electrical tape to create a winding road on a shower curtain. Place the curtain on the floor and encourage students to use scrap paper and recyclable materials to make their own city and country landmarks, such as trees, lakes, farms, houses, skyscrapers, parks, and buildings. Then provide toy cars, tractors, and two toy mice to use with the road map. Encourage a group of youngsters to use the materials to make up a sequel to the story.

Where Is That Gingerbread Man?

Students' understanding of directions will be off and running with this exercise. Show your youngsters the compass rose on a map. Explain that its purpose is to indicate direction. Reinforce the concepts of north, south, east, and west by duplicating page 75, cutting the cards out, and taping them to the wall as indicated at the right. Trace the lens of a flashlight on dark-colored tagboard and cut it out. Then cut out a small gingerbread man from the center of the tagboard circle. Tape the circle over the lens of the flashlight as shown.

After rereading the gingerbread tale, darken the room. Have youngsters join you in singing the song below. At the end of the tune, shine the flashlight at one of the four directional signs. (You'll need to be no more than a few feet away from the signs.) Encourage youngsters to respond by naming the specific direction. Continue playing as interest allows.

(sung to the tune of "Oh Where, Oh Where Has My Little Dog Gone?")

Oh where, oh where is the Gingerbread Man?
Oh where, oh where can he be?
Is he north or south
Or east or west?
Oh where, oh where can he be?

"Beary" Good Directions

Continue to challenge your young learners with cardinal directions by using this activity page. Make a copy of page 76 for each child. Explain that the Three Bears family needs help getting through the forest and to the members' specific destinations. Read aloud each of the directions below; then pause, giving youngsters a chance to follow them. We're right on track!

Directions
1. Use a red crayon to trace a path from Baby Bear south to the stop sign and then west to the schoolhouse.
2. Use a blue crayon to trace a path from Mama Bear north to the gate and then west to the apple tree.
3. Use a green crayon to trace a path from Papa Bear east to the bridge and then south to the fishing hole.

The Three Bears' Blueprints

The idea that many maps depict a bird's-eye view is often a difficult concept for youngsters to understand. Try this nifty notion to introduce the idea of perspective and spatial relationships. In advance, gather a camera, film, and dollhouse furniture. Arrange the furniture on a tabletop; then take a picture of it from above. Rearrange the floor plan and take another snapshot. Continue rearranging and photographing until you have several different furniture groupings. Place the photos, furniture, and a sturdy step stool in a center. Invite a student to arrange the furniture to match each photo. Then have him climb the stool to check his work. Reward efforts with a big bear hug!

Red Riding Hood's Romp

Hit the trails and head for Grandma's house to discover some truths about distance. Mount a large house cutout to a classroom wall. Then use three different colors of tape to make three paths on the floor: one straight, one curvy, and one zigzag. (Make sure the straight path *looks* longer than the other two but that it is actually the shortest path.) Have your youngsters predict which path is longer. Then have small groups of students work together to measure the length of each path with yarn, linking cubes, or other nonstandard units of measurement. Were the predictions correct? Which path would *you* want to take if the Big Bad Wolf were chasing you?

Whose Shoe?

This follow-up to *Cinderella* will send youngsters on a mysterious tour of the school. To prepare, draw a simple map of the school on a sheet of chart paper. Then arrange for a well-known staff member to knock on your closed classroom door and leave one of his shoes. When you go to the door, act shocked to find the shoe. Then line up your little ones and start looking for the shoe's owner. Stop frequently and ask which way you should go; then have a different volunteer mark the class's path on the school map. When the owner is found, invite him back to the classroom to read a silly version of the Cinderella tale, such as *Dinorella: A Prehistoric Fairy Tale* by Pamela Duncan Edwards or *Cinder-Elly* by Frances Minters.

Fee, Fie, Foe, Fum!

Teaching youngsters map skills sure is fun! This closing activity is sure to be worth its weight in gold. In advance, hide several paper bags filled with gold foil-wrapped candy in different locations on the playground. Make separate maps, each one disclosing the location of a different bag and taking a different route to get to the playground. Read *Jack and the Beanstalk* to your class. Then divide your students into as many groups as you have treasure bags. Assign each group a map and an adult helper. Will they be as lucky as Jack?

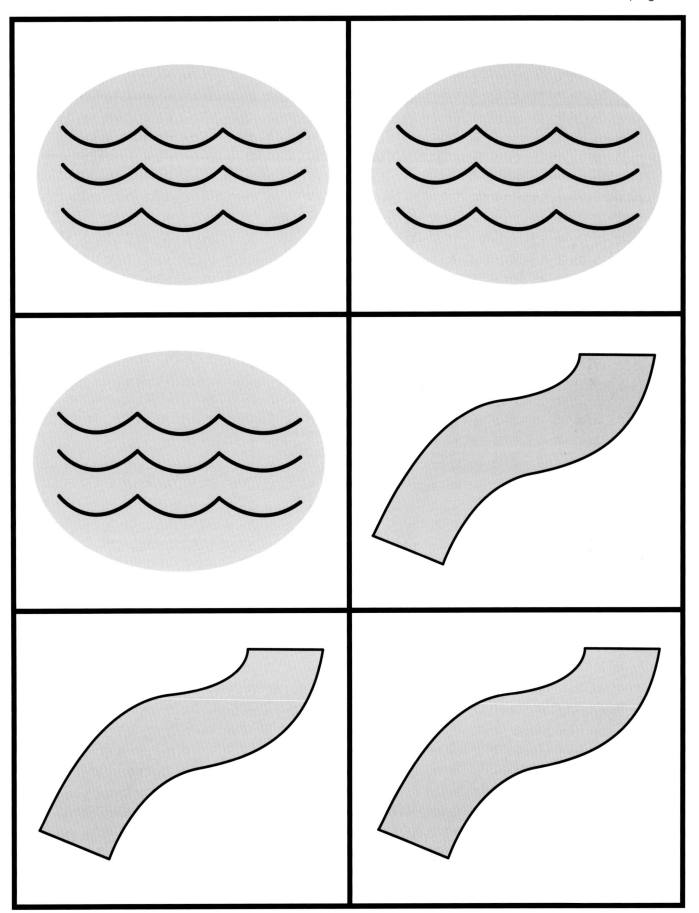

Game Cards

Use with "The Race Route" on page 70.

north

east

south

west

Name

"Beary" Good Directions

Listen.

Draw.

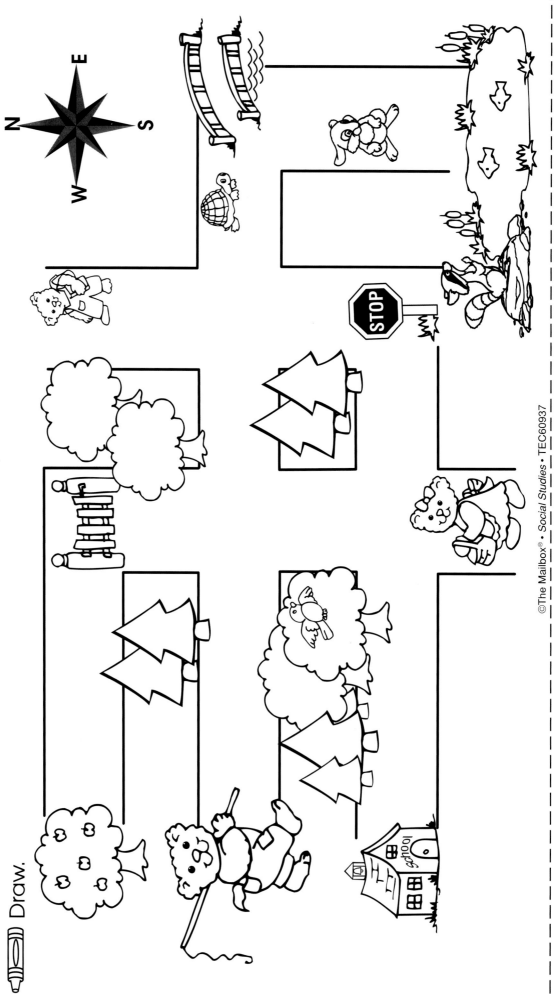

Note to the teacher: Use with "'Beary' Good Directions" on page 71.

Transportation

Keep on Truckin'

Rev up your students' engines with a collection of ideas that will keep them truckin'.

In advance, send a note home with each child inviting him to bring a toy truck to school. In the note, ask parents to label the truck with the child's name. Have a few extras on hand for students who do not own one.

The Truck Show

A whole lot of learning goes on at this classroom truck show! Give your little ones the opportunity to show off their trucks and practice math skills with these simple circle-time ideas. Allow each youngster, in turn, to tell about her truck. Then have the children sort the trucks in a variety of ways, such as by color, number of wheels, size, and whether the truck makes noise. After each sort, have students graph the groupings and then discuss the results. Next, instruct students to order the trucks by placing them in a line from smallest to largest. Then have students count the total number of wheels for the entire collection. Now that's the way to truck through some math skills!

Kathy Etringer—Gr. K
Reinbeck Elementary
Reinbeck, IA

Load 'em Up

Your youngsters load up on some counting and fine-motor practice when they complete this activity. In advance, purchase ten plastic trucks that have an open back for carrying items. Cut index cards to equal the size of each truck's tailgate. Program each card with a different numeral from 1 to 10. Tape one card to the tailgate of each truck. Place the trucks, a pair of tongs, and a container of items, such as cotton balls or Lincoln Logs toys, at a center. Invite each child to count as he uses the tongs to load each truck with the correct number of items. When the trucks have been filled, have the student count backward as he removes the items from each truck. That's 5, 4, 3, 2, 1, done!

Kathy Thomure—Gr. K
Creative World School, Inc.
Raytown, MO

Truck Driver Song

There's no need to turn on the radio while your students are truckin' along. Just teach them this little trucker song sung to a familiar tune.

(sung to the tune of "I'm a Little Teapot")

I'm a little trucker, see me go.
Sometimes I drive fast and sometimes slow.
When I see friends I honk to say, "Hi";
Then I wave and drive right on by!

Kathy Etringer—Gr. K
Reinbeck Elementary
Reinbeck, IA

My truck carries oranges.
It has stripes on it.
By Sydney

A New Paint Job

Look for racing stripes on these truck paintings and you'll probably see some! In advance, program a class supply of white construction paper sheets as shown. Lead students in a discussion of the different shapes that could be used to paint a truck. Demonstrate this by painting a truck using circles, squares, and rectangles. Then invite each child to paint a truck. After the paint has dried, help each student complete the sentences on her paper. Hang the paintings on a bulletin board and title the display "Super Shape Trucks."

Kathy Etringer

Classroom Raceway

Students, start your engines! This fun game will help your youngsters develop motor skills. Place two strips of tape on the floor three to four feet apart. Label one strip of tape "Start" and the other strip "Finish." Have students hold their trucks and make a single file line behind the starting line. Instruct each child, in turn, to push his truck toward the finish line. Write the child's initials on a small piece of tape and use it to mark the place where the truck stopped. Then have the child remove his truck from the raceway. Continue in this manner until each child has had a turn. The winner of the race is the child who pushes his truck the closest to the finish line without going over it. Welcome to the winner's circle!

Kathy Etringer

Cruisin' Across the Curriculum

Get moving with these activities that hook up transportation
with loads of cross-curricular learning.

ideas contributed by Kristine Puls

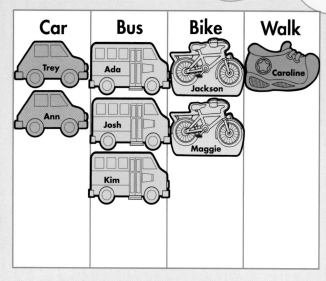

Car	Bus	Bike	Walk
Trey	Ada	Jackson	Caroline
Ann	Josh	Maggie	
	Kim		

Traveling to School

Get your transportation study on the road by inviting young-sters to share how they travel from home to school. To prepare, duplicate the pattern from page 83 that best depicts each child's mode of transportation. Cut out the patterns. Also make extra patterns for those students who travel to school using several different means of transportation. Then program a sheet of chart paper labeled to correspond to each mode of transportation used.

Read aloud *This Is the Way We Go to School: A Book About Children Around the World* by Edith Baer. Encourage students to discuss the many different ways children around the world get to school. Then have each child tell how he travels to school. Ask him to select a pattern that corresponds with his mode of trans-portation and write his name on it. Then have him tape his pattern in the appropriate column on the chart. Discuss what the completed chart reveals.

Going Places

Invite youngsters to travel through a storm—a brainstorm, that is—on their way to creating a transportation big book. In advance, duplicate the bus pattern (page 83). Enlarge the pattern and trace it on two large sheets of construction paper; then cut out each vehicle to make the book covers. For the book pages, trace around the cutouts on large sheets of white construction paper and cut along the resulting outlines. Then collect magazines containing an assortment of vehicle pictures.

Prompt your students to brainstorm a variety of modes of transportation. Write student responses on the backs of the book covers. Then have each child glue magazine cutouts of different types of transportation onto her page. Or invite her to illustrate her choice of transportation. Stack the completed pages between the two book covers, with the brainstormed lists on each cover facing inside the book. Bind the book along the edge; then write the title "Going Places" on the front cover. Place the book in your reading center for students to cruise through during their reading time.

jet boat
yacht wagon
plane canoe
helicopter skates
car

Movin' Along

Give your students a real ride to observe the world of transportation around your community. In advance, make arrangements for some form of transportation for your class—vans, a bus, a commuter train, or any travel combination. Plan a route that will give students the opportunity to witness a variety of travel forms. For instance, your route might take the class past a lake, across a railroad track, near an airport, and into the streets of town. As you travel, encourage youngsters to be on the lookout for forms of transportation. Ask them to point out vehicles and identify where they travel—on land, in water, or in air. Take along an instant camera to take snapshots of the many different forms of trans-portation observed. After returning to the class, have youngsters use the photos (or their own drawings) to create a display depicting where each form of transportation travels. Title the display "Movin' Along."

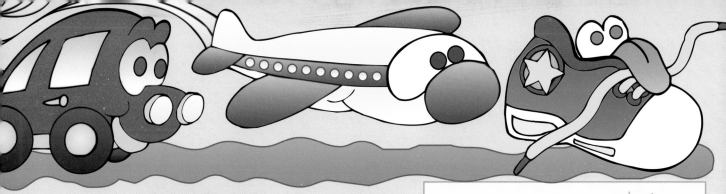

Land Travel

Show off different kinds of land transportation with a special exhibit. In advance, arrange to have parents, coworkers, car dealers, or other resource persons provide different types of land transportation for your exhibit. Some show-entry suggestions include cars, trucks, bikes, wagons, skates, sleds, strollers, motorcycles, and recreational vehicles. (If your school's space or resources prevent having an exhibit of real vehicles, you might ask students to bring in toy models.) On the day of the show, pair each student with a volunteer—perhaps an older student or an adult helper. Give each pair a sheet of paper and a pencil. Ask the volunteer to record comments and observations made by the student while they visit the exhibit. Encourage students to note the features of each vehicle such as its wheels, the seats, its size and shape, and whether or not it uses an engine.

It has one seat, but someone can sit on the back.   Tanner

After returning to class, give each child several sheets of construction paper. Have the child and his partner refer to his page of comments as he illustrates a different type of land vehicle on each page. Ask his partner to write the child's dictation on the corresponding page. Bind each child's pages between two sheets of construction paper. Write his dictated title on the front cover; then exhibit the books in the media center or other prominent places for other students, teachers, and parents to read.

Carol A. Parent—Pre-K, Washington Christian School, Silver Spring, MD

The Airplane Song

Teach this song to youngsters to heighten their enthusiasm for learning about airplanes.

(sung to the tune of "Take Me Out to the Ballgame")

Take me out to the airport.
Take me up to the gate.
Buy me a ticket to fly so high.
I want to fly through the big, open sky!
Let me zoom, zoom, zoom! See, I'm soaring
Above cars and buses and trains.
For it's great to fly through the sky on a big airplane!

A Convoy of Sounds

Round up the trucks—we're gonna have a convoy! Youngsters will be riding in high gear when they make initial-letter-to-sound hookups with this truck convoy. Enlarge the truck pattern on page 84; then duplicate the pattern on construction paper as many times as the desired number of letter-sound association pairs. Cut out each truck; then cut apart each cab from each trailer. Glue a picture on the trailer side of the truck. Write the corresponding first letter on the cab section. (If desired, program the backs for self-checking.) Then laminate the truck sets. To use, have a child match each trailer to a cab by pairing the picture's initial sound with its corresponding letter. Now that's a big ten-four, good buddy!

The Wild Blue Yonder

Youngsters' imaginations will soar when they create their own flying machines. Provide a cardboard box for every two or three students. Prepare each box by turning and taping the top and bottom flaps inside the box. Then gather scraps of poster board and a variety of items that can be used to create instrument panel gadgets, such as spools, an assortment of plastic lids, and clock stamps and stamp pads.

Encourage students to discuss the many different types of vehicles that fly. For inspiration, provide illustrations from a book such as *Airplanes and Flying Machines* by Pascale De Bourgoing and read aloud *Flying* by Donald Crews. Then invite each group of students to use the provided materials to make any kind of flying machine. Help the groups, as necessary, cut and attach materials. Afterward, invite students, in turn, to pilot their machines on imaginary flights—over cities, mountains, the sea, the jungle, or even the North Pole. After each flight, ask the pilot to share something about his trip.

Magnetic Tugboat

While students learn about the mighty power of a tugboat, they can also be introduced to the power of a magnet. Enlarge the tugboat and ship patterns on page 84; then make one tugboat pattern and a supply of ship patterns on construction paper. Cut out and laminate each pattern. Punch a hole near the back of the tugboat; then thread a length of yarn through the hole and tie it securely. Tie the other end of the yarn around a magnet. Gather a variety of objects—include some objects that will and some that will not be attracted to a magnet. Glue or tape a different object to the end of each of the ship cutouts. Then have youngsters sponge-paint a harbor scene on a length of bulletin board paper. Guide them to paint the docks, piers, and warehouses on the right half of the paper. Then explain to students that a tugboat is used to move ships, many of which are much larger than the tugboat. Place several ships along the left half of the harbor scene. Invite a child to move the tugboat past the ships one at a time, passing the magnet over the item attached to the ship. If the item is attracted to the magnet, ask the child to "tow" the ship to a dock on the right side of the harbor. Afterward, discuss the results of your youngsters' towing efforts.

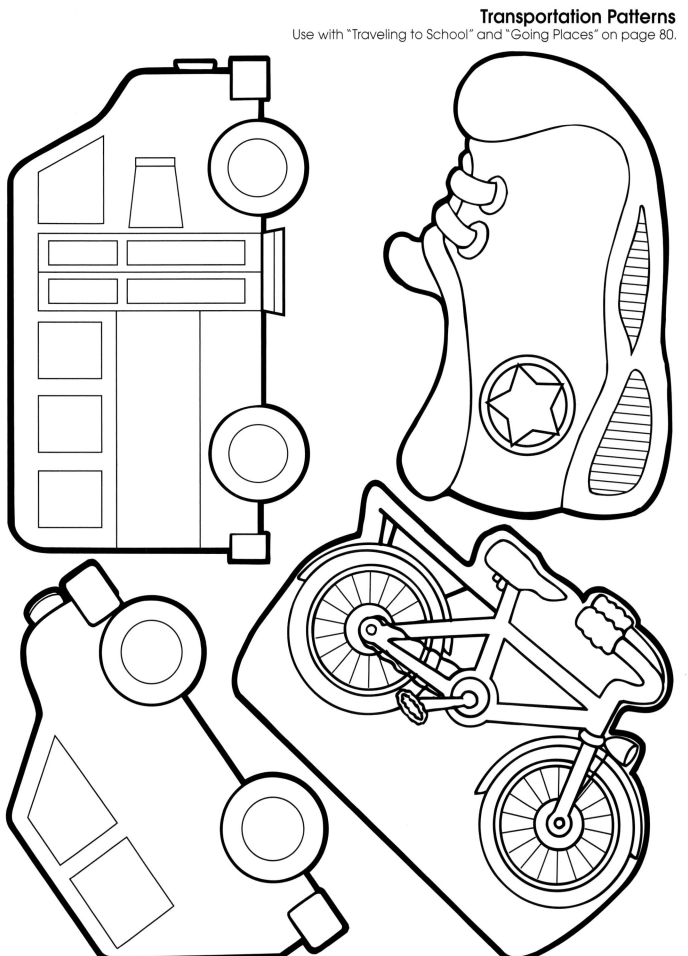

Truck and Boat Patterns

Use with "A Convoy of Sounds" on page 81 and "Magnetic Tugboat" on page 82.

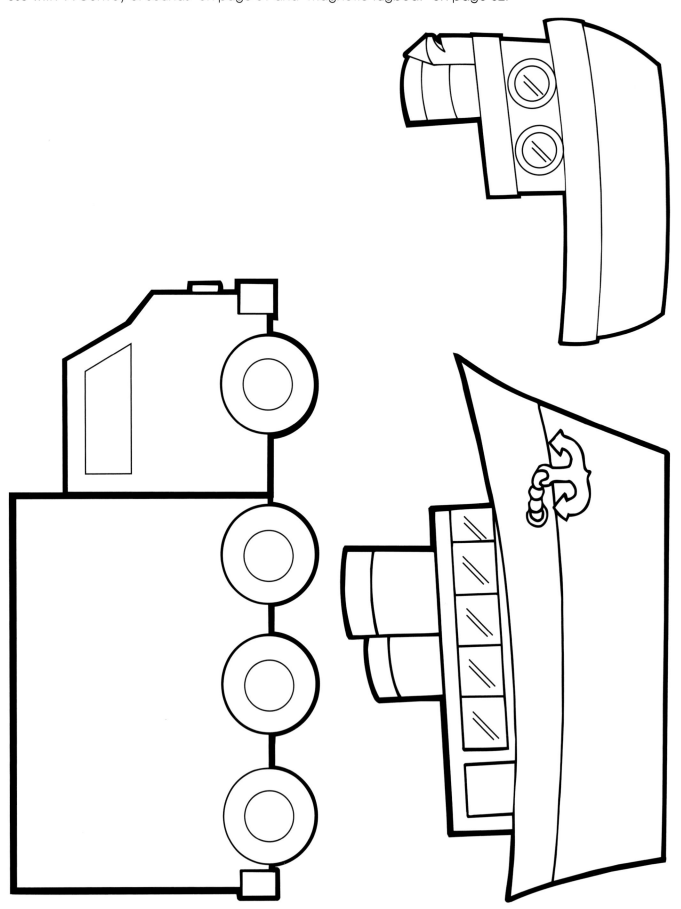

Patriotism

Hooray for the USA!

It's time to start celebrating America! The 21 days from Flag Day (June 14) to Independence Day (July 4) have been declared by Congress as a period to honor our country. So use the following activities to help instill a little patriotic pride into young hearts and minds.

Salute Lady Liberty

Each of your students will be carrying a torch for the famous Lady Liberty when he creates this patriotic project! To begin, show students a photo of the Statue of Liberty from an encyclopedia or nonfiction book. Share several facts about the statue (see the list shown) to familiarize youngsters with this famous American symbol. Then help each child follow the directions to make a torch of his own. It's a lot like Lady Liberty's!

Materials for one torch:
9" white paper plate
¾ paper towel tube
green, white, and blue tempera paints
orange or yellow tissue paper
pencil

paintbrush
glue
masking tape
scissors

Teacher preparation:
Mix the green, white, and blue paints to get a seafoam green color.

Directions:
1. Cut around the rim of the plate to form points.
2. Stand the paper towel tube on end in the center of the plate and use a pencil to trace around it. Then cut out the circle.
3. Fit the tube into the circle and secure it with strips of masking tape.
4. Paint the entire torch; then allow the paint to dry.
5. Cut three or four rectangles from the tissue paper. Gather the rectangles together and push one end of them into the top of the tube. Use glue to secure the paper.
6. Crumple and twist the remaining ends of the tissue paper to resemble flames.

Margaret Southard—Gr. K, Cleveland, NY

Statue of Liberty Facts
- Construction of the statue began in 1875. The statue was completed in France in 1884. Almost a year later, the statue arrived in New York Harbor.
- From the base to the torch, the statue is more than 151 feet tall.
- To give an idea of the statue's size, her nose is 4¾ feet long and her index finger is eight feet long.
- To visit the Statue of Liberty, you have to travel by ferry to Ellis Island in New York Harbor.

With my hand on my heart,
That's how I start
The Pledge of Allegiance, you see.

I say I'll be true
To the red, white, and blue
And America, land of the free!

Ask me to recite the
Pledge of Allegiance for you!

The Pledge of Allegiance

Your students have probably been reciting the Pledge of Allegiance since the beginning of the year. But do they know what the words mean? Inform your youngsters that the Pledge of Allegiance is a promise to be loyal and true, both to our country's flag and to the USA itself. Demonstrate the proper way to stand when reciting the pledge—with the right hand over the heart. Snap an instant photo of each child standing this way, preferably with the classroom flag in the background. Copy a certificate from page 88 for each child. Have the child color her certificate and then attach her photo where indicated. Teach your students the poem on the certificate to remind them of the pledge's meaning. Then send the certificates home to stimulate some patriotic discussions!

Ada Goren, Winston-Salem, NC

Where's the White House?

What do you get when you take a popular party game, give it a patriotic twist, and sprinkle in some factual information? You get a game of Pin the White House on the Map! To prepare, duplicate the White House patterns on page 89 to make a class supply; then cut out the patterns. Attach a large map of the United States to a classroom wall. You'll also need a bandana (or another type of blindfold) and some Sticky-Tac.

Working with one small group at a time, gather around the map and give each child a White House cutout. Have the child write her name on the back of her cutout and then add a bit of Sticky-Tac. Explain that this game is similar to Pin the Tail on the Donkey, with the object being to stick the White House on the map as close to Washington, DC, as possible. Point out Washington's location on the map and then have the first player take her turn. During the game, share the interesting facts below. Your students will soon be experts on the executive mansion! Award a small prize to the child whose White House is closest to the nation's capital. Then give each of your players a patriotic sticker for participating.

Ada Goren, Winston-Salem, NC

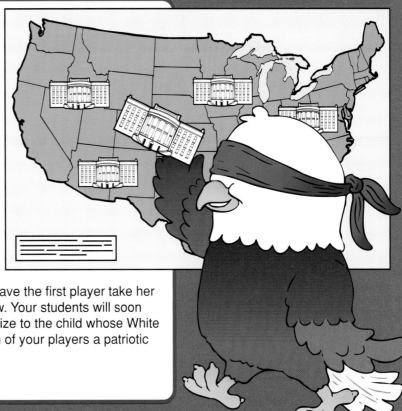

White House Facts
- Although George Washington oversaw the building of the White House, our second president, John Adams, was the first to live there.
- The Oval Office, located in the White House, is where the president works.
- The Red Room and the Green Room are rooms in the White House. They were named for the colors of their walls.

I'm proud to be an American because. . .

I can go to church anywhere.

Proud to Be an American!

Bring your mini unit to a star-spangled ending with this display! To prepare, make a class supply of the hat pattern (page 89) on white construction paper. Then, for each child, program the top of a sheet of 12" x 18" construction paper with "I'm proud to be an American because…" Encourage each youngster to decorate his hat using red and blue crayons, glitter, foil stars, and patriotic stickers. Then instruct him to cut out his hat and glue it below the programming on his sheet of construction paper as shown. Have him draw a full-body portrait of himself wearing the hat. Below the child's drawing, invite him to write (or dictate for you to write) an ending to the programmed sentence. Then display the finished projects on a bulletin board trimmed in red, white, and blue. Let's hear it for the USA!

Taryn Lynn Way—Gr. K, Los Molinos Elementary School
Los Molinos, CA

Certificates

Use with "The Pledge of Allegiance" on page 86.

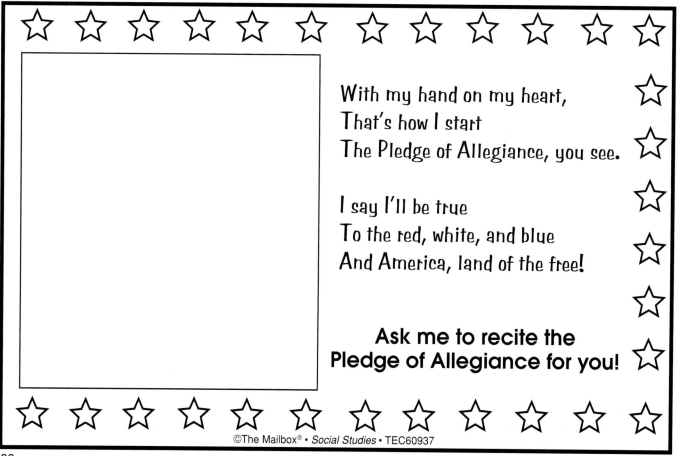

With my hand on my heart,
That's how I start
The Pledge of Allegiance, you see.

I say I'll be true
To the red, white, and blue
And America, land of the free!

**Ask me to recite the
Pledge of Allegiance for you!**

©The Mailbox® • *Social Studies* • TEC60937

With my hand on my heart,
That's how I start
The Pledge of Allegiance, you see.

I say I'll be true
To the red, white, and blue
And America, land of the free!

**Ask me to recite the
Pledge of Allegiance for you!**

©The Mailbox® • *Social Studies* • TEC60937

White House Patterns
Use with "Where's the White House?" on page 87.

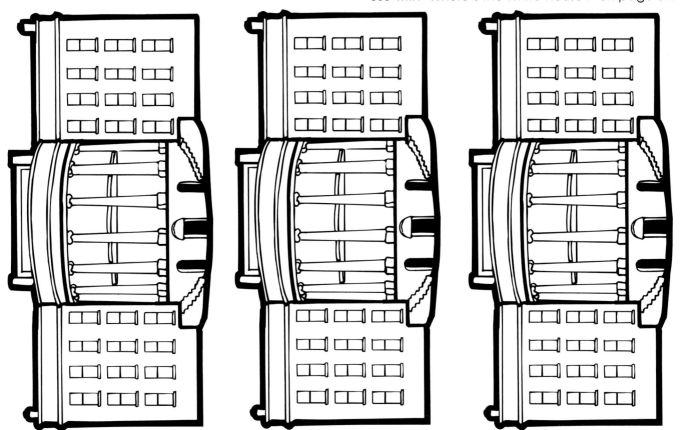

Hat Patterns
Use with "Proud to Be an American!" on page 87.

Red, White, & Blue Review

With Independence Day just around the corner, strike up the enthusiasm in your classroom with this cross-curricular red, white, and blue review!

ideas contributed by Rachel Meseke Castro

I Love Red, White, and Blue

Your little ones will be rallying around the flag after learning this upbeat song. Write the song below on chart paper. Before you teach the song, encourage students to carefully examine your classroom flag. Prompt them to talk about the colors, shapes, and patterns that they see. Then introduce the song, encouraging students to sing along as they are able.

(sung to the tune of "When the Saints Go Marching In")

Our flag is red.
Our flag is white.
And in the corner it is blue.
Oh, our flag stands for our country.
How I love red, white, and blue!

Some stripes are red.
Some stripes are white.
And in the corner it is blue.
Oh, our flag stands for our country.
How I love red, white, and blue!

Patriotic Painting

Fly those colors high in your classroom with these red, white, and blue projects. To prepare, gather several marbles, a 9" x 13" cake pan, white construction paper, and a shallow dish (each) of red and blue paint. To do this activity, have a child place a sheet of white construction paper in the cake pan. Then direct her to take a marble and roll it in the red or the blue paint. Next, have her drop the marble in the cake pan and roll it around the paper by moving the cake pan. Have the child repeat this process (with red and/or blue paint) as often as she likes. When the paint is dry, mount the painted paper on a sheet of red or blue construction paper. Display the finished projects in your classroom for all to see.

Ice Plot

Here's a red, white, and blue graphing activity and a cool treat all in one. In advance, prepare a graph with a column each for red, white, and blue. Then give each child a red, white, and blue Bomb Pop ice pop. As they enjoy their treats, ask children to notice which colors they like the best. Then have each child write her name on a sticky note and attach it in the appropriate column. Afterward, discuss what the graph reveals. Is it red, white, or blue for you?

Stars and Stripes Forever

This red, white, and blue center provides lots of patriotic patterning practice. To make the center, use a paper cutter to cut out a large supply of three-inch-long construction paper stripes in red and white. Also cut out a classroom supply of blue 4" x 18" construction paper strips. Then use scissors or a die-cutter to cut out a large supply of white stars. Place all of the cutouts in a center along with some glue sticks. When a child visits this center, have him use the blue strip as a background. Then encourage him to arrange and glue the stars and stripes in the pattern of his choice. When each child has designed a pattern, have him share his pattern during a group time. Save all the pattern strips to use in "We've Got the Rhythm" on this page.

We've Got the Rhythm!

After your class has made the pattern strips in "Stars and Stripes Forever," use them for this activity involving movement, sound, and rhythm. As a class, decide on a movement or sound for each symbol in the patterns. For example, you might clap for each red stripe, stomp your foot for each white stripe, and say, "Hurray!" for each star. Then show one pattern strip and have your class perform it together. After your children catch on, they can change the sounds and motions as often as they like. This is great fun as a whole-class activity or even just to fill a spare minute or two.

Flag Day is on June 14.

It is celebrated on that date because June 14, 1777, is the day the first American flag was chosen.

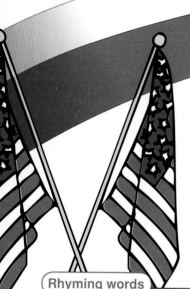

Positively Presidential

Celebrate Presidents' Day, the third Monday in February, by using this patriotic selection of books and activities.

ideas by Rhonda L. Chiles

Rhyming words

Meet George Washington
Written by Patricia A. Pingry
Illustrated by Stephanie McFetridge Britt

With simple text and nice illustrations, this informative book details the life of George Washington and introduces students to the man who would become our first president.

After reading the story, invite each child to make a George Washington wand. To prepare, cut out a small black construction paper silhouette of Washington for each child. Cut red, white, and blue ribbon into eight-inch lengths for each student. To make a wand, have each child glue one end of each ribbon together and then glue the silhouette on top. Next, help each youngster staple the silhouette and ribbons to the end of a straw. Read the information below and have students think of a body part whose name rhymes with the last word in each bulleted point. Then reread the points and have youngsters use their wands to touch each corresponding body part.

- George Washington grew up on a farm.
- George Washington fought in a war with the army he led.
- A very brave soldier Washington proved to be.
- He helped win the war, and there was no more fear.
- George Washington became the first president of our land.

Reading Writing

A Picture Book of Thomas Jefferson
Written by David A. Adler
Illustrated by John and Alexandra Wallner

Introduce your students to Thomas Jefferson with this book, which provides an interesting account of the many accomplishments of our third president.

Share this informative book with your class. Discuss with students that Thomas Jefferson felt it was important to set aside time every day to read and write. Then review Jefferson's accomplishments of being a farmer, author of the Declaration of Independence, governor, vice president, president, and inventor. Plan a special reading and writing time with your class in honor of Thomas Jefferson. Have each child write or dictate something she has learned about Thomas Jefferson and then illustrate her thought. Invite each student to share her paper with the class. After each child has shared, demonstrate how to roll the paper up and tie it with a length of ribbon. Encourage each youngster to read and write each day, just like Thomas Jefferson. You never know—you might be nurturing future presidents of our great country!

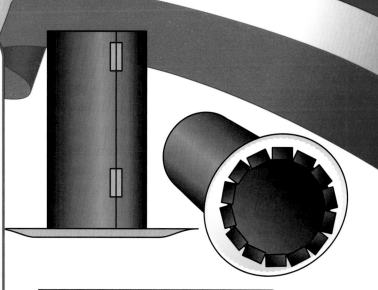

Abe Lincoln's Hat
Written by Martha Brenner
Illustrated by Donald Cook

Students are sure to enjoy this delightfully descriptive book about our 16th president and his tall black hat. Your youngsters will find out that Mr. Lincoln wore his hat for reasons other than just covering his head!

Lead students to discuss what important things they would store in Abraham Lincoln's hat. For each child, cut a six-inch circle from the center of a nine-inch paper plate to make a hat brim. Have each youngster paint both sides of his brim black. While the paint dries, give each child a 12" x 18" sheet of black construction paper and have him make one-inch cuts along one long side. Assist each student in forming the paper into a tube and taping it to his brim as shown. Encourage him to slide his important papers from the day into his hat, wear it home, and share the information he has learned about President Lincoln's special hat.

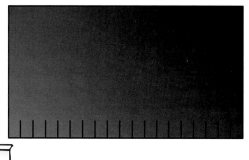

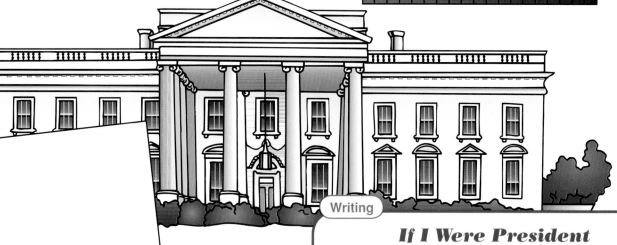

If I were president, I would_____

If I were president, I would mAK SUYE ALL PEOPLE GAd food

If I Were President
Written by Catherine Stier
Illustrated by DyAnne DiSalvo-Ryan

Our president is a very busy person! This informative book details the duties of our president by describing them through the eyes of a child.

Let the presidential speeches begin! Review the story and talk about the duties of the president. Then have students brainstorm a list of things they would do as president. Next, make a class supply of page 95. Distribute the papers and have each student design a poster showing what her platform would be as president. Then have her write or dictate an ending to the sentence on her paper. Display the posters on a bulletin board titled "Look Out, White House—Here We Come!"

Woodrow, the White House Mouse

Written by Peter W. Barnes and Cheryl Shaw Barnes

President Woodrow G. Washingtail, an endearing mouse, is the main character in this book, which describes the president's job. The book includes charming illustrations showing various rooms in the White House.

Have your youngsters entertain at the White House and practice math facts at the same time. Make a copy of page 96 for each child. Discuss with students the following White House facts: The president and his family live in the White House. The White House has 132 rooms. Three rooms have color names. The Red Room has red silk on its walls; it is used for small parties. The Blue Room is an oval room where the president meets guests. The Green Room has green silk on its walls. It is a parlor, like the Red Room. Next, give each student a copy of page 96 and ten half-inch gray pompoms to represent the mice from the story.

Have students color the rooms of the White House appropriately. Then say aloud math problems using the characters' names, such as "Place President Washingtail in the Green Room. Have George and Art go to the Green Room too. How many mice are in the Green Room all together?" Have students manipulate the pom-poms to calculate each math problem. Way to move those mice!

Arthur Meets the President

Written and Illustrated by Marc Brown

Tickle your little ones' funny bones with this humorous tale of Arthur and his friends traveling to Washington, DC. Arthur wins an essay contest and is invited to speak at the White House. Will he forget his speech in front of the president?

Lead students to discuss the things they can do to help make America great. After the discussion, invite each child to make a presidential snack in honor of the people who have served as the president of the United States. Gather the ingredients and materials below and then guide each child to complete her special snack. Yummy!

Ingredients for one:
graham cracker (four sections)
vanilla frosting
M&M's Minis candies

Utensils and supplies:
plastic knife per child
paper plate per child

Directions:
1. Spread frosting on a graham cracker.
2. Add M&M's Minis candies to form the number of presidents there have been.

Name ______________________________

If I were president, I would ______________________

____

____

Note to the teacher: Use with *If I Were President* on page 93.

Name _____

Listen and do.

Green Room

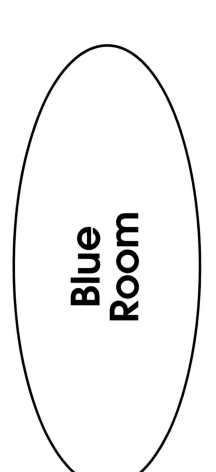

The White House

Red Room

Blue Room

Note to the teacher: Use with *Woodrow, the White House Mouse* on page 94.

Holidays and Celebrations

Thanksgiving

Thanksgiving is a time for friends, family, food, and fun. But it's also a time to remember our long-celebrated Thanksgiving friends—the Pilgrims and Native Americans. Use the ideas in this unit to teach your youngsters about the history of one of our most beloved American holidays.

ideas contributed by Allison Ward

Telling the Tale

The story leading up to the very first Thanksgiving is certainly a tale worth telling! Share the history of Thanksgiving with your children by reading Ann McGovern's *The Pilgrims' First Thanksgiving*. The simple text and realistic illustrations introduce youngsters to the trials and triumphs leading up to that historic day. If this title isn't available, check your library for a similar realistic fiction book. Then tell the tale!

The Mayflower

Making a *Mayflower*

Hoist the sails on creativity as children design a rich dramatic-play experience. After sharing the story of the first Thanksgiving (see "Telling the Tale"), invite small groups of children to share in creating a classroom *Mayflower*. Begin with a large box. Encourage groups of children to paint the outside of the box to resemble the *Mayflower*. (Keep your collection of Thanksgiving books handy for children's reference.) Then encourage student groups to use art supplies to create the ship's details (see the illustration). This ship will launch youngsters on hours of Thanksgiving dramatic play!

Jennifer Miller—Grs. K–1 Special Education, Alann Elementary School, Reston, VA

Mayflower Menu

Mealtime on the *Mayflower* was no picnic—so to speak! Since there was no refrigeration on the ship, the Pilgrims had to bring food that would not spoil during the long journey. Give your youngsters just a sampling of *Mayflower* fare. When you share another realistic Thanksgiving book, serve your children beef jerky, hard cheese, and crackers. Invite each child to snack on these *Mayflower* foods while you read. Afterward, ask children for their comments. Not bad for a day or two? How about 66 days?

Remembered

Packing Pilgrims

What would you take to a brand-new land if you were traveling on a very crowded ship? Pose this question to your children, reminding them that the Pilgrims were going to a land where there would be no refrigerators, houses, or stores. In fact, they were going to a wilderness! Encourage each child to imagine that she is a Pilgrim and illustrate one thing that she would pack to bring on the ship. (If desired, suggest realistic ideas from the list below.) Then have each child cut out her illustration and glue it to the inside of your classroom *Mayflower*. By the way, did you know that one *Mayflower* passenger brought along 126 pairs of shoes? Of course, he shared!

On Board the Ship

sacks of cabbages, turnips, dried peas, flour	tools
barrels of salted meat, smoked fish	books
rounds of cheese	farm animals
seeds	two dogs
gardening tools	one cat
cookware	

Jennifer Miller—Grs. K–1 Special Education
Alann Elementary School, Reston, VA

Ship Shape

With a little creative artistry, these *Mayflower* look-alikes take on fine form. To make one ship, photocopy the ship pattern (page 102) on brown construction paper. Cut out the pattern; then place it on a large sheet of blue paper. Arrange one end of each of three craft sticks behind the ship (to resemble masts). Next, cut out an assortment of sail shapes from paper, wallpaper, or fabric scraps. Then glue all the pieces in place. Use these ships for the activity described in "What's in a Name?"

What's in a Name?

Most researchers think that the *Mayflower* was named after the pretty white flower that grows on the hawthorn tree and blooms in May in England. These researchers also think that there was probably a picture of that flower painted on the *Mayflower*. After discussing this with your children, encourage each child to think of a meaningful name for her own ship (made in "Ship Shape"). Then have her draw a picture, cut it out, and glue it onto her ship. Also invite each child to use markers to add colorful details to her ship if desired. Then have each child hold her finished project and "sail" it in front of her as you all sing "Sail, Sail, Sail Our Ship" (on page 100). Encourage youngsters to take their finished projects home and share the whole Thanksgiving story and song with their families.

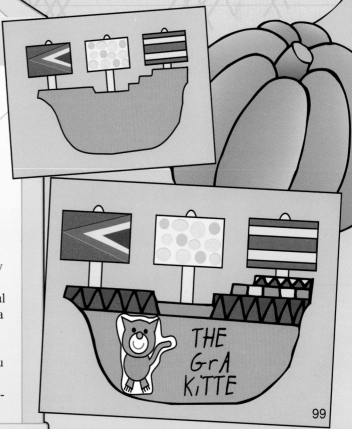

Sail, Sail, Sail Our Ship

Here's a little sailing song that your pretend Pilgrims might like to sing as they journey at sea.

(sung to the tune of "Row, Row, Row Your Boat")

Sail, sail, sail our ship
Across the deep blue sea.
We're sailing to America
Where we can all be free.

Thanks, Squanto!

Corn chips, corn dogs, cornflakes, corn bread—where would we be without corn? And more to the Thanksgiving point, where would we be without Squanto? Squanto was a Native American who spoke English. After he met the Pilgrims, he decided to stay with them and help them survive in the new land. Among many other important things, Squanto taught the Pilgrims how to grow corn. Without this corn, the Pilgrims would have starved. So take a moment to recognize Squanto with this creatively corny art project. Stock your art area with colored and regular popcorn kernels, popped popcorn, tagboard pieces, and craft glue. Encourage each child in the center to squeeze a glue design onto a piece of tagboard. Then have him arrange the popped popcorn and the kernels along the glue lines. When the glue is dry, back each creation with another color of tagboard. Then mount all the projects on a board titled "Thanks, Squanto!" Encourage your little ones to share Squanto's story with classroom visitors.

Three Days of Thanks

After the Pilgrims' first very difficult winter in the new land, they were so thankful to be alive and to have a bountiful fall harvest that they celebrated for three days in a row! After explaining this to your youngsters, launch three days of thanks in your classroom. To prepare, cut out a large butcher paper basket and mount it on a board titled "Thinking Thankful Thoughts." Then enlarge and make a supply of the food patterns on page 103 on colorful construction paper. Prompt children to begin thinking about what they are thankful for in their lives. On the first of your chosen three days, have each child choose a food cutout and write or illustrate a thankful thought on it. Then help him mount it in the basket. Repeat this activity on the second and third days, creating an overflowing display of thankful thoughts.

Are Ye Ready? Are Ye Set?

Eating wasn't the only thing going on during that first Thanksgiving celebration—there were lots of fun and games too! Running races and tug-of-war are two activities that have held people's interest from way back then until now. This year, when you take your youngsters out for a few running races and a couple of rounds of tug-of-war, add a touch of the old days to the festivities. To start off each game or race, call out, "Are ye ready? Are ye set? Go!"

Pumpkin Delight

Although pumpkin pie is standard fare for Thanksgiving these days, historians think that the pie might not have been around until a couple of years after the very first Thanksgiving. So if you're planning to have a classroom feast, try adding this form of pumpkin to your menu. First, cut the top off a baking pumpkin. Then have your youngsters help remove the seeds and pulp. Next, fill the pumpkin with apple chunks, raisins, walnuts, and cranberries. Sprinkle the filling with cinnamon and sugar, and dot with butter. Replace the pumpkin top and bake the pumpkin on a cookie sheet at 350° for approximately 1½ hours. To serve, scoop out the warm fruit as well as the pumpkin. Mmm…delightful!

Pam Crane

I wd liK to milK a got.

I can sit down to eat.

Looking Back

Get your modern-day pilgrims pondering the past with this thought-provoking activity. To set the stage, read aloud a book that realistically depicts life in the new land. Some especially good choices include *Sarah Morton's Day, Samuel Eaton's Day,* and *Tapenum's Day* by Kate Waters. Photographed in full color at Plimoth Plantation—a living history museum—these books accurately offer an up-close look at different children's days in 17th-century America.

After sharing the book(s), prompt your students to brainstorm a list of activities in which children participated in those early days. Write their comments on chart paper. Then give each child a large sheet of construction paper and ask her to fold it in half. On one half, encourage each child to write about and illustrate one thing from the past that she wishes she could do in the present. On the other half, have her illustrate one thing that she is happy she can do now. Bind all the pages between construction paper covers titled "Now and Then." Invite each child to share her page with the group. Ah, this is the life…or was that?

Ship Pattern

Use with "Ship Shape" on page 99.

©The Mailbox® • Social Studies • TEC60937

Winter Celebrations

Use this collection of ideas to introduce and celebrate a variety of winter holidays and special occasions.

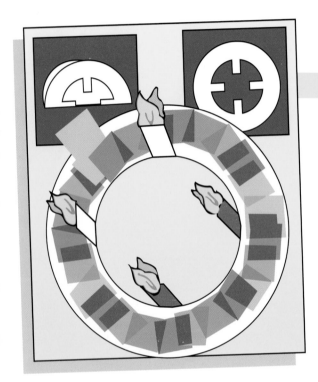

Luciadagen Crowns

In Sweden, St. Lucy's Day is widely celebrated as Luciadagen. The name Lucy means "light," and St. Lucy became known as a symbol of the preciousness of light. Traditionally, this occasion is observed by dressing the family's oldest daughter in a white robe, a crimson sash, and a leaf-covered crown of candles. On the morning of December 13, she and other costumed children awaken their family members with a tray of coffee and pastries.

Commemorate this Swedish celebration by making Luciadagen crowns. Photocopy the patterns on page 107; then cut them out to make tracers. To make a crown, fold a nine-inch paper plate in half. Place the straight edge of the tracer on the center of the fold and trace around the rest of the shape. With the plate still folded, cut along the lines to cut out the interior shape—the candles. Next, color the wreath and the candles. Then glue on pieces of torn tissue paper to represent leaves on the wreath and flames on the candles. When the crown is dry, fold the candles back so they stand up. Then invite each child to wear her decorative head wreath as she serves herself a pastry from a tray passed from child to child.

Michelle Weeks—Gr. K, Oxford Middle School, Oxford, AL

Dreidel Match

Provide background information about a widely observed Jewish holiday by sharing Leslie Kimmelman's informative *Hanukkah Lights, Hanukkah Nights.* Then show your students one element of the traditional holiday festivities—a dreidel. (If you don't have a dreidel, *Let's Play Dreidel!,* a book/cassette/dreidel set, is published by Kar-Ben Copies, Inc., and is available to order by calling 1-800-4-KARBEN.) Next, reinforce your youngsters' visual-discrimination and memory abilities with this small-group dreidel-matching game. To prepare, duplicate the dreidel cards (page 108) on construction paper; then mount the cards on tagboard. Laminate the cards. Then arrange all the cards facedown on a table. Invite a player to turn over two cards. If the cards match, the child keeps them, and play moves to the next player. If the cards do not match, have the child return them facedown on the table. Continue play with the next player until all the matches have been found.

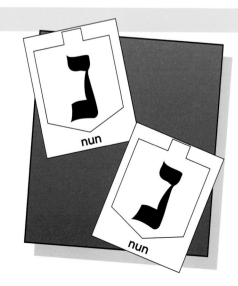

Colorful Kwanzaa Mats

These colorful Kwanzaa mats are decorative reminders of the colors and meanings of Kwanzaa. In advance, collect a class supply of light-colored carpet samples (many carpet stores or outlets will donate these). Also gather sponge-tipped ink bottles (such as bingo daubers) in red, green, and black. Then cut out a different shape from each of several squares of sturdy cardboard or tagboard. Before introducing this craft, read aloud *The Gifts of Kwanzaa* by Synthia Saint James. Afterward, discuss the Kwanzaa colors and their meanings—black for the people, red for their struggles, and green for hope.

Then have youngsters make these decorative mats to help them remember the special Kwanzaa colors and their meanings. Give each child a carpet sample and have him position a cardboard stencil on his carpet. Encourage him to dot the ink bottle over the shape's opening to transfer that design onto the carpet. Then have him reposition the cardboard and transfer the design again, this time using a different ink color. Invite the child to continue decorating his carpet in this manner, using all three Kwanzaa colors. Set the completed mats aside to dry; then have each student take his mat home and share the principles of Kwanzaa with his family.

adapted from an idea by Connie Mangin—Special Education
Brillion Elementary, Brillion, WI

Kwanzaa Lights

Candles play an important role in the Kwanzaa celebration. Seven candles are placed in a candleholder called the *kinara*—three red, one black, and three green. On the first night of Kwanzaa, the black candle is lit. On each night thereafter, an additional candle is lit—alternating red and green until the entire kinara is glowing on the final night of Kwanzaa. To recognize this special celebration, youngsters will enjoy creating these sparkling Kwanzaa candles. For each child, cut out seven tagboard strips to represent candles. Also, for each child, cut a wide strip of brown tagboard to represent the kinara. In three separate containers, mix equal amounts of warm water and sugar; then stir the mixtures until the sugar dissolves. Add a different Kwanzaa color of tempera paint to each container. Then have each child paint his tagboard candles with the solutions. After his candles dry, have the child glue them along the top of his kinara. Then invite him to top each candle with a glued-on, torn tissue paper flame.

Peace Ringers

To celebrate the birthday of Dr. Martin Luther King Jr., youngsters can follow his example and ring out the message of peace. First, introduce this honored man and his beliefs by reading aloud *Happy Birthday, Martin Luther King* by Jean Marzollo. After discussing the book, ask children to brainstorm ways in which people can live together peacefully. Then have each child write/dictate her response on a strip of paper. Punch a hole in one end of the paper strip. Next, have each child decorate the bottom side of a small paper plate half. Help her thread a thin ribbon through the loop of a jingle bell; then tie a knot approximately 1½ inches above the bell. Wrap the plate around the ribbon just above the knot, stapling the straight edges of the plate together to create a cone. Thread one end of the ribbon through the hole in the paper strip; then tie the ends of the ribbon together. Invite each child to read her statement of peace to the class and then ring her peace bell for all to hear.

We can live together in peace if we help each other.   Abbey

105

St. Basil's Cake

In Greece, the first day of the new year is known as the Feast of St. Basil. Celebrations for this occasion actually begin on New Year's Eve, when it is believed that St. Basil gives his blessings to the people, animals, and belongings of each home and also brings presents to the children. On January 1, a special cake with a coin baked into it—the *Vassilopita*—is served. The person who finds the coin in his slice of cake is considered to be the luckiest family member for the new year.

Introduce your students to this Grecian custom with individual versions of the Vassilopita. To make these cakes, bake a class quantity of cupcakes according to the package directions. After the cupcakes cool, use a knife to cut a deep slit in the middle of each one. Slip a gumdrop or candy-coated chocolate into the slit; then spread icing over the tops of the cupcakes. Encourage each child to announce when he discovers his hidden surprise. Then remind him of all the good luck that awaits him in the new year.

Lions on Parade

Chinese New Year begins in late January or early February and includes outdoor parades and fireworks. A Lion Dance is performed to scare away evil spirits and to bring good luck for the new year. Youngsters will enjoy creating lion masks for their very own classroom Lion Dance.

In advance, read aloud *Lion Dancer: Ernie Wan's Chinese New Year* by Kate Waters and Madeline Slovenz-Low. Then give each child a paper plate that has two eyeholes cut out of it. Have him color his mask; then invite him to decorate his mask by gluing on a variety of craft items, such as colorful feathers, sequins, pom-poms, and paper scraps and streamers. After the glue dries, help each child tape a wide craft stick securely in place. Then play some lively music while youngsters use their masks and perform their own versions of the Lion Dance. Your little lions will have a roaring good time.

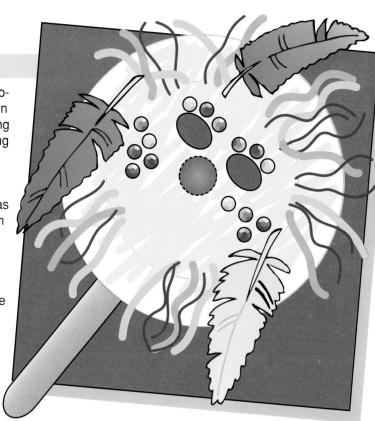

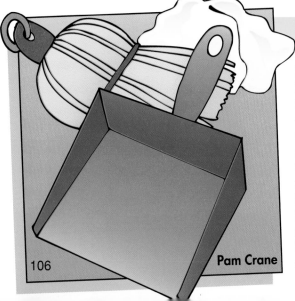

A Clean Start

The most popular holiday celebration in Japan is the new year festivities that take place from January 1 to 3. On this occasion, the Japanese engage in ceremonial housecleanings, visits, and gift exchanges. To celebrate the new year Japanese-style, hold a ceremonial classroom cleaning. Gather a number of cleaning supplies, such as brooms, dustpans, carpet sweepers, dusters, buckets, festive-shaped sponges, and mild detergents. Attach ribbons or bows to the handles of the cleaning tools. Partially fill the bucket with soapy water. Then invite each child to select some cleaning supplies and an area of the room to clean. Provide a ceremonial atmosphere by playing instrumental music while the children are working. When the cleaning is done, have students bring their cleaning supplies to group time. Light a scented candle; then hold a ceremony in which each child returns her cleaning supplies to be stored. After putting away all the supplies, dedicate the classroom to a fresh, clean start for the new year.

Pam Crane

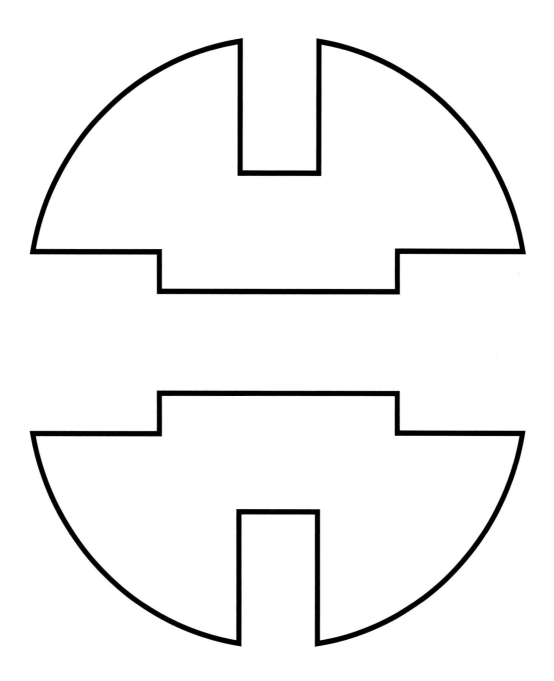

Dreidel Cards

Use with "Dreidel Match" on page 104.

nun

gimmel

hay

shin

nun

gimmel

hay

shin

nun

gimmel

hay

shin

nun

gimmel

hay

shin

Cinco de Mayo

Although the fifth of May is not Mexico's Independence Day, it is a very important holiday for many Mexicans and Mexican Americans. This day marks an incredible victory gained by the Mexican forces in 1862 over a larger and better-equipped French army. This victory is still celebrated today for the great unity and patriotism it kindled in the Mexican people.

Use the ideas that follow during the first week of May to help educate your little ones about Mexican heritage and culture. Then encourage them to celebrate Cinco de Mayo with their families on May 5. Olé!

MATH

UNO, DOS, TRES

Introduce your youngsters to Spanish number words by reading a counting book such as *Count Your Way Through Mexico* by Jim Haskins. Then help students create these counting booklets to take home. Duplicate pages 111 and 112 for each child. Have her cut out the number words along the dotted lines. Then help her glue each word to the appropriate page. Next, invite the child to color and then cut apart the booklet's pages. Then have her sequence the pages, staple them together along the left side, and sign her name on the front cover. Now let's count in Spanish!

Linda Masternak Justice
Kansas City, MO

Uno, dos, tres...

MATH

CUATRO, CINCO, SEIS

Count on this game to reinforce the Spanish number words. Label a class set of construction paper squares each with a different number from 1 to 10. Tape the squares to the floor in a circular arrangement. Then play some mariachi music and invite your students to dance around the circle. After a brief period of time, stop the music and instruct each child to stand on a different square. Call out a number in Spanish; have the children standing on that number go to the middle of the circle. During the next round of play, instruct this group to collectively decide on the number to call out next. Then, when the music stops again, encourage them to call out the number and rejoin the dance. Keep on counting!

Rachel Castro
Albuquerque, NM

WHAT TO WEAR?

Get into the spirit of Cinco de Mayo with these fun-to-wear accessories that your children can make. A *poncho* is a blanket that has an opening in the middle for a person's head and drapes over the shoulders. Ponchos have colorful patterns and are often handwoven. They are worn during cold and rainy weather. Make a simplified version of a poncho by folding a five-foot length of bulletin board paper in half and then cutting an opening along the fold for the head. Decorate the paper with colorful paints, markers, or stamps. If desired, fringe-cut the edges of the paper.

Sombreros are wide-brimmed hats made of straw or felt that some Mexicans wear to protect themselves from the sun. To help youngsters make a paper variation of this hat, provide a tagboard pattern similar to the one shown. Have each child trace this pattern on a large sheet of tagboard and then cut it out. Encourage him to use crayons, markers, and sequins to decorate his hat. Then cut a slit through the middle of the brim to fit the child's head. Once the ponchos and sombreros are complete, the fiesta can begin!

poncho idea by Nancy Goldberg
B'nai Israel Schilit Nursery School
Rockville, MD

sombrero idea by Helaine Donnelly—Gr. K
Washington School
Plainfield, NJ

Cut here.

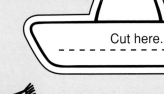

GRAND OLD FLAGS

Bring in a Mexican flag and an American flag to spark some critical thinking. Draw a blank Venn diagram on the chalkboard or on a sheet of chart paper. Then display the two flags side by side. Have youngsters discuss the similarities and differences between the flags. List their responses in the appropriate places on the diagram. Are the flags more alike than different? Conclude the activity by having each child name something she likes about each flag.

Alison LaManna—Grs. K–5 ESL
Warrenville, IL

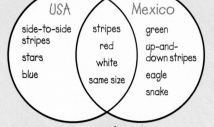

USA — side-to-side stripes, stars, blue
(shared) — stripes, red, white, same size
Mexico — green, up-and-down stripes, eagle, snake

GIVE IT A FLING!

Bullfighting is a popular spectator sport in Mexico. As a matter of fact, the biggest bullring in the world is located in Mexico City! Amateur and professional bullfights are often held during fiestas. While gathering participants for bullfighting may be difficult, you won't have any trouble rounding up your youngsters to play this game.

Enlarge a simple bull's head pattern and trace it onto poster board; then cut it out. Mount the bull's head onto the side of a cardboard box. Then cut the centers out of five paper plates, leaving the rims intact, to make rings. Label each ring with a different number from 1 to 5.

Set the bull, the rings, paper, and a pencil in a center. To play, each child in a pair throws the set of rings at the bull's horns. Then she totals up the numbers on the rings that are caught on the horns to calculate her score. The first player to score 20 wins the game. What a fun way to take addition practice by the horns!

Rachel Castro, Albuquerque, NM

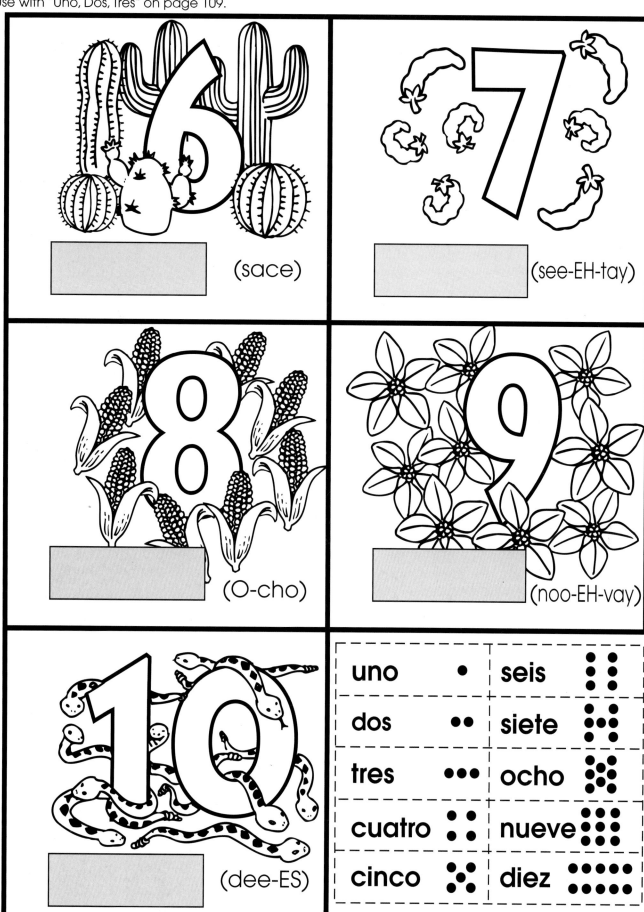

6 (sace)

7 (see-EH-tay)

8 (O-cho)

9 (noo-EH-vay)

10 (dee-ES)

uno	•	seis	
dos	••	siete	
tres	•••	ocho	
cuatro		nueve	
cinco		diez	

LET'S COUNT!

by _____

©The Mailbox® • *Social Studies* • TEC60937

(OO-no)

(doce)

(trace)

(KWA-tro)

(SING-ko)